The Zapple Diaries

The Zapple Diaries

The Rise and Fall of the Last Beatles Label

Barry Miles

PETER
OWEN

This Peter Owen Publishers edition is published by arrangement with
Elephant Book Company Limited

PETER OWEN PUBLISHERS
81 Ridge Road
London N8 9NP

First published in Great Britain 2015 by Peter Owen Publishers

© 2015 Elephant Book Company Limited

Editorial Director: Will Steeds
Project Editor: Joanna De Vries
Art Editor: Paul Palmer-Edwards, Grade Design Consultants

ISBN 978-0-7206-1860-0

A catalogue record for this book is available from the British Library

Printed and bound in China

Contents

ZAP

ZAP!!

Prequel: From Apple to Zapple

APPLE WAS CREATED IN 1967 to bring the Beatles' enter-prises together for tax purposes, so that instead of paying nineteen and sixpence in the pound the Beatles paid only sixteen shillings (there were twenty shillings in the pound). The original directors were Clive Epstein, Alistair Taylor, Geoffrey Ellis, a solicitor and an accountant, and the idea was that they would quietly announce to the tax authorities that they would be opening a string of shops. Alistair Taylor told American author Geoffrey Giuliano: 'That was the original idea and when the boys heard about this they decided this could be boring, they didn't really want their name above a string of shops. The original idea was greetings cards. Imagine Beatles greetings cards shops! They didn't like that at all. Gradually they started drifting in on meetings and Apple Corps really evolved from there. Later it turned into this silly philosophy.'[1] John Lennon was suitably scathing:

> Clive Epstein or some other such business freak came up to us and said you've got to spend so much money, or the tax will take you. We were thinking of opening a chain of retail clothes shops or some barmy thing like that . . . and we were all thinking that if we are going to open a shop let's open something we're interested in, and we went through all these different ideas about this, that and the other. Paul had a nice idea about opening up white houses, where we would sell white china and things like that, everything white, because you can never get anything white, you know, which was pretty groovy, and it didn't end up with that, it ended up with Apple and all this junk and The Fool and all those stupid clothes and all that.[2]

Clive Epstein, Brian's brother, worked in the financial administration side of the New End Music Stores (NEMS), Epstein's management company, and set to work. On 19 April 1967 the Beatles became a legal partnership sharing all their income, whether from group, live or solo work (except songwriting) and The Beatles and Co. Ltd was created to bind them together legally for ten years on a goodwill share issue of £1 million. The first anyone in the public would have known of it was on 19 May 1967, with the launch of *Sgt Pepper's Lonely Hearts Club Band*, which had a discreet green apple on the back sleeve. On 17 November The Beatles Ltd changed its name to Apple Music Ltd, and Apple Music Ltd became The Beatles Ltd. With Apple Music up and running, they began signing up artists. Grapefruit was the first, and John and Paul attended their first recording session, held at IBC Studios on Portland Place, on 24 November 1967. The band wasn't actually signed until 11 December. John named them Grapefruit after the book of the same name given to him by Yoko two months earlier. Most of the group were former members of Tony Rivers and the Castaways, one of Brian Epstein's groups.

Rather than the proposed chain of card shops, the Beatles instead opted to open a clothes boutique, to be run by The Fool, three Dutch designers and an English publicist, who were anything but fools. Paul was having a fling with one of them. The shop opened on 7 December 1967 and closed seven months later on 31 July; the Beatles having decided that they did not want to be involved with the rag trade. The Beatles and their staff and friends helped themselves to the clothes, then the public were let in to take anything they wanted for free – one item each.

Apple's first office was above the boutique, then shortly afterwards they moved to more permanent, although still temporary, offices at 95 Wigmore Street on 22 January. The choice of Marylebone as a location was Paul McCartney's: he knew the area well from living for several years in Wimpole Street in the house of his then girlfriend

Jane Asher. Apple's appointed A&R man, Peter Asher, also lived there in Weymouth Street, so it was convenient for both of them.

On 12 January 1968 Apple Music Ltd, which had been in business since June 1963 as The Beatles Ltd, changed its name yet again, this time to Apple Corps Ltd, and The Beatles Film Productions Ltd changed its name to Apple Films Ltd. Apple Corps in turn controlled dozens of new companies: Apple Records Ltd, Apple Films Ltd, Apple Music Publishing Ltd and Apple Electronics Ltd; soon to be joined by Apple Wholesale Ltd, Apple Retail Ltd, Apple Television Ltd, Apple Publicity Ltd and more. The Apple School never got off the ground; it would have been run by Ivan Vaughan, an old friend who first introduced John and Paul to each other.

Neil Aspinall spent weeks incorporating these companies and registering them as trademarks in every country in the world where it was possible to do so. This paid off in spades when Apple Computers launched the iPad and moved into music distribution. A series of lawsuits netted the Beatles many millions for copyright infringement.

A record company needs a logo, and so Neil Aspinall, now managing director of Apple Corps Ltd, contacted Gene Mahon, a graphic designer from Dublin who had worked on the *Sgt Pepper* cover, laying out the back sleeve which contains the lyrics – the first time anyone had ever printed the lyrics on an album sleeve; usually you had to buy them from a sheet-music publisher. It also showed Paul McCartney with his back to the viewer. Neil told Gene that he needed a photograph of an apple to use on the centre label of Apple records. Gene immediately had the brilliant idea of using a photograph of an apple on the A-side of the record, with no writing or information, and on the B-side using a photograph of an apple sliced in half, to give a white background to all the relevant label copy for both sides. The left-hand side of the apple would be headed 'This Side' with the title of the track, the artist, the running time, the publishing and copyright information; the right-hand side would be headed 'Other Side' and would give the same information for the A-side.

Gene commissioned Paul Castell to photograph a series of apples: red apples, green apples and sliced apples against different coloured backgrounds. Two days later they had an assortment of 2¼-inch transparencies of apples against red, blue, black, green and yellow backdrops. Gene selected the two he thought were the best but included the others for consideration. It turned out that it was a legal requirement for copyright to list the contents on both sides of the record, so that idea was out. Meetings were held and slides of various apples were projected on to office walls. Batches of eight-inch by ten-inch colour prints were made, six at a time, one for each Beatle and one each for Neil Aspinall and Ron Kass, the head of Apple Records. Eventually they decided upon a nice shiny green Granny Smith on a black background. Alan Aldridge, former chief designer for Penguin Books who was to publish *The Beatles Illustrated Lyrics*, was brought in to draw the copyright lettering that surrounds the outer perimeter of each record. The finished artwork was sent to New York where the dye transfers were made from which all the labels would be printed. It had taken six months.

Apple had become a fully functioning company. I was not involved in the early days; I joined towards the end of 1968, but the staff stayed more or less the same until Allen Klein came in and fired everyone. John Lennon, Paul McCartney, George Harrison and Ringo Starr were the presidents of the company; Neil Aspinall, their former roadie, became managing director (he had previously trained as an accountant); Alistair Taylor, from NEMS, was the general manager and Mr Fixit; Peter Brown, who had been with Brian Epstein since the early days, was made a director and was the Master Mr Fixit and the Beatles' personal assistant. Peter Brown's own personal assistant was Joanne Newfield, who had previously been Brian Epstein's personal assistant until he died. Harry Pinsker, the head of Bryce Hanmer accountants, became a director; Peter Asher was appointed head of A&R with Chris O'Dell as his personal assistant; Malcolm Evans, the Beatles' roadie, was made assistant managing director; Derek Taylor was made director of public relations and had a staff of seven, not all of them paid; Alexis Mardas, 'Magic Alex', the former television repair man, became head of Apple Electronics; Denis O'Dell was head of Apple Films; Ron Kass left his job as president of Liberty Records to become head of Apple Records, one of the most important figures in the place. There were maybe twenty other directors and staff, running the various Apple divisions. Accountant Harry Pinsker and four of the other directors resigned in protest against John and Yoko appearing nude on the sleeve of *Two Virgins*, not from prudery – there's not much of that in the record business – but because they saw it as damaging to the Beatles' image.

The way the companies were set up meant that all the directors resigned each year and were reappointed. When Klein moved in, he made sure that Peter Brown and Neil Aspinall were not reappointed. Klein could not believe that they were not all motivated by greed and the desire to be the most powerful man in the company, but they weren't; most of them were motivated by misplaced loyalty to the Beatles – they would do anything for them, working incredibly long hours to achieve the impossible and receiving scant praise for doing so. As can be seen above, Apple was a typical sixties company: all the bosses, without exception, were men, and all the secretaries were women, and without the women very little would have ever been done there.

The Beatles had encountered strong opposition to the sleeve of *Sgt Pepper* from EMI – on the grounds of cost – and felt that EMI were out of touch with them and with the youth record market. Apple was seen as a way of controlling their own 'brand' as it would now be called. All along they had wanted to release more controversial and experimental material – John and Yoko's *Two Virgins* being the best example, which EMI had refused point-blank to distribute – and the Zapple division was created specifically to do this.

Chapter 1

'Z' Is for Zapple

Before Apple: Ringo Starr, George Harrison and John Lennon share a joke with an unknown man outside Teddington Studios, west London, in 1964.

The Beatles performed regularly at Teddington, most memorably in February 1964, when they arrived by boat to appear on the *Big Night Out* show and were ferried from the riverside in an open-top Porsche; the boys were flying high that night after their success in the USA, paving the way for their future transatlantic music and business adventures.

'Z' Is for Zapple

EARLY IN SPRING 1968 Apple Records placed advertisements in the music press written by Derek Taylor that read:

'A' is for Apple, 'Z' is for Zapple. Introducing Zapple, a new label from Apple Records.

For about a year now Apple has been producing pop records. And it's done quite well too, with artists like Mary Hopkin, Jackie Lomax and, of course, the Beatles.

Many people have asked, why don't we try something different for a change? Enough pop is enough, they've said.

Well, we don't want Apple to become a 'one-product company' any more than anyone else does.

So we've done something about it.

This something is called Zapple.

What's Zapple about?

We want to publish all sorts of sounds. Some of these sounds will be spoken, some electronic, some classical. We'll be producing recorded interviews too. Some of the people we put on record will be well known, some not so well known.

This means that you'll get plenty of variety. We don't want Zapple to become a one-track record label.

We'll publish almost anything providing it's valid and good. We're not going to put out rubbish, at any price.

What will Zapple cost?

We decided to divide the Zapple label into three price categories. These prices will depend by and large on the contents and production costs of the album. If the album doesn't cost much to produce then you won't pay much. The three price categories are as follows:

15/- (ZAP)

21/- (ZAPREC)

37/5 (ZAPPLE)

The first two Zapples will be out May 26th.

One's by John Lennon and Yoko Ono. It's called 'Life with the Lions: Unfinished Music No. 2'.

The other's by George Harrison. It's called 'Electronic Sound'. This is a new thing for George. It's all done on a machine called the Moog Synthesizer. One side's called 'Under the Mersey Wall'. The other's called 'No Time or Space'.

The third Zapple album will be by American poet Richard Brautigan. It'll be called 'Listening to Richard Brautigan'. We're hoping to release it soon along with one other, which we've yet to decide on.

Where to buy Zapples.

Zapples should be on sale in most leading record shops and some bookshops. If you're not sure what a 'leading' record shop is and whether there's one near you, fill in the coupon below and pop it in the post to us.

Not only will we tell you where to get hold of a Zapple but we'll keep you informed about future Zapples.

Our future Zapples will include records by Lawrence Ferlinghetti, Michael McClure, Charles Olson, Allen Ginsberg and American comedian Lord Buckley.

So listen to Zapple. It's something else again.

The advertisement ended with a coupon giving Jack Oliver's name and the address of Apple at 3 Savile Row. In the USA Jack's address was given as 1750 North Vine, Hollywood, Calif. 90028, the address of the Capitol Tower, the US subsidiary of EMI Records, distributors of Apple and Zapple records.

Zapple's roots went back even earlier than those of its parent company Apple. It came from a Paul McCartney project back in the winter of 1965–6.

I knew Paul from the Indica Books and Gallery project. I had been the manager of Better Books, on Charing Cross Road, an avant-garde bookshop that specialized in French film, modern poetry, experimental art and theatre. There were film shows and poetry readings including one by Allen Ginsberg and another by Lawrence Ferlinghetti that I organized. The owner, Tony Godwin, had decided to sell it and move to New York, and it looked as if the avant-garde and experimental sides of the shop would cease to be. I decided to start my own bookshop and almost immediately connected with artist and critic John Dunbar, who was looking to start his own art gallery. It seemed obvious that we should combine forces, and John brought in an old friend of his, Peter Asher, who provided the initial money for the venture. Peter was one half of Peter and Gordon, a successful duo who had recently had a number-one hit in both the USA and the UK. Together we formed a company called Miles, Asher and Dunbar Ltd (MAD) and began to look for

Top: Peter Asher stands outside Indica during the construction period. The cloth in the window was put up to stop people looking in at Paul McCartney, who helped to paint the walls and put up shelves.

Bottom: Peter walks away from the crowd towards the camera, while playing host outside an Indica private-view party in Mason's Yard. The gallery became known for its cutting-edge exhibitions, and those 'in the know' flocked to its private parties.

premises that would be suitable for both an art gallery and a bookshop. Indica Books and Gallery (yes, it was named after *Cannabis indica*) was started in August 1965 on £2,000, of which Peter Asher put in £1,400 and I put in £600 worth of books; I had an arrangement with Tony Godwin to buy stock from him at a trade discount and to be able to order books from publishers using his account. He had sold Better Books and approved very much of the idea of Indica and wanted to help us as much as he could.

In the meantime I began to assemble the stock for the bookshop in the basement music room of Peter's parents' house at 57 Wimpole Street. Peter still lived at home then, as did his sister, the actress Jane Asher. Peter had an L-shaped room on the top floor, and in the smaller room next door (once a maid's room), directly above Jane's bedroom, lived Jane's boyfriend, Paul McCartney. He had been there for several years, ever since the Beatles moved to London from Liverpool in 1963. Paul took an immediate interest in the book stock, and sometimes, late at night, when he got in from a club or a gig, he would browse through the books and leave me a note to say which ones he had taken. He was Indica's first customer.

John Dunbar found premises next to The Scotch of St James's, a club in Mason's Yard, off Duke Street, St James's. This was the appropriate area for the gallery because it was where the few modern art galleries that London had were located, one or two streets either side of Piccadilly. Paul McCartney yet again took an active role, preparing the walls, filling in holes with polymer filling, painting walls and helping put up the shelves. We had to whitewash the windows to stop crowds gathering to watch. Peter reported that Paul had been behaving in a suspicious way and would not let anyone into his room. We joked that he must have a groupie holed up in there. Then, on the day the bookshop opened, Paul pulled up in his Aston Martin and heaved a large, heavy package out from the back seat. He had designed and had printed wrapping paper for the shop – 5,000 sheets of it. He had hand-lettered the name and address of the shop in black and white and composed them in the shape of a Union Jack – very sixties. It was a terrific gift, and he was correct in thinking that we had not thought to provide ourselves with wrapping paper, so it was very welcome.

In addition to the books I assembled in the music room, I also lent Paul magazines and books: *Big Table* magazine from Chicago, *Evergreen Review* from New York, *New Departures* from London, *Paris Review* and the like, all featuring Beat Generation or avant-garde work by Samuel Beckett, John Cage, Jack Kerouac, Cornelius Cardew, William Burroughs, Jean Genet and their circle. He enjoyed *At Swim-Two-Birds* by Flann O'Brian and *Ubu Roi* by Alfred Jarry.

In those days it was Paul who was the avant-garde one. While John Lennon stayed at home in the stockbroker belt, Paul and Jane Asher attended premières and first nights; Jane had been a child actress and knew a large number of film and theatre people. Through Indica Gallery Paul met artists such as Takis and bought one of his 'Signals' – a red-and-blue light mounted on thin metal wands, person-height. Inspired by Paul, John and George also bought one. Unimpressed, Ringo had his chauffeur knock one up in the workshop of his garage. Paul called them 'Peter and Gordon' because the red light was the shorter of the two (Peter had red hair) – typical Beatle irreverent humour. Gallery owner Robert Fraser introduced him to a number of his artists, including Peter Blake and Eduardo Paolozzi, and he bought examples of their work. He attended private views of Claes Oldenburg and Richard Hamilton, and on one occasion Fraser took Andy Warhol round to Paul's house and they screened *Chelsea Girls* for him and a bunch of friends using two projectors; Paul was impressed that Warhol didn't seem to be particularly bothered about getting the two projectors in sync.

At my flat Paul listened to Blue Beat records (Shenley Duffus, 'Duck Soup' by Drumbago, the Charms, Derrick and Patsy, Prince Buster and the All Stars) as well as John Cage's *Indeterminacy* – a set of texts, some longer than others but all read aloud by Cage in two minutes: for some he had to read very quickly, others very slowly. One crowd-pleaser, after a few joints, was a two-volume Folkways recording of a ceremony held in a Japanese Zen monastery. One track consisted of a bell that rang once a minute; the build-up of tension waiting for the bell to ring was palpable and the relief immediate and hilarious. I had a lot of records by Albert Ayler on ESP and Danish Debut, Pharoah Saunders, the two ESP recordings by Sun Ra and his Solar Arkestra, Ron Blake and the controversial (at the time) *Free Jazz* album by the Ornette Coleman Double Quartet: thirty-eight minutes of spontaneous collective inspiration by two reeds, two bassists, two drummers and two trumpets. It was this album that inspired Paul to suggest that if you were in complete control of your consciousness you would be able to differentiate between audio sounds so completely that you could release a record with Beethoven on the left stereo and the Beatles on the right, playing simultaneously. He said:

> I remember one of our ideas was to master two records on to a thing and all you would do in the future was, you'd just switch out one of them with your brain. You'd say, 'I'm not listening to the Beethoven, I'm listening to the Beatles', but they would be both going on. So this was . . . cheap, cheerful, good value for money. You had to be able to switch one of them out.[1]

He was sure that the brain was capable of deciding which one to listen to and had the ability to flip between one and the other: in other words, a typical sixties stoned conversation. Other favourites included the IBM 7090 computer singing 'Bicycle Made for Two' and Luciano Berio's electronic music compositions based on speeded up and collaged tape-recordings. In Paul's own words, he was walking around town 'with his antenna out' absorbing information and ideas, filing them away for future use. Of course he was also imparting information; I learned far more about music listening to him talk and explain then he did from browsing his way through my record collection.

Paul's reaction to the experimental literary magazines I lent him was to envisage an audio equivalent. One September evening in 1965 Peter Asher and Paul were visiting me and my wife Sue at our flat in Hanson Street. We were talking about how difficult it was for people to find out what was happening at the experimental end of the arts when Paul suggested an audio magazine that would come out monthly or even fortnightly, and instead of a review of a poetry reading or a book there would be a recording of the reading or the author reading from the book. The idea would be for an editor to gather in recordings of all that month's most interesting cultural activity, be it a scientific lecture or an obscure performance at the Wigmore Hall. Paul said:

> Instead of reading in *Melody Maker* that there was a great jam session down the Bag O'Nails and that Eric Burdon and Georgie Fame were playing together, there would be a recording of it . . . We could even have really important things from the BBC Third Programme that people might have missed. Have it available on subscription as cheap as it possibly could be. We should be able to put it out really cheap, what with the vast resources of EMI and NEMS![2]

It was all very exciting. The problem was that none of us had time to actually do it. Between Peter and myself we could have edited it without too much trouble, but, as to actually making all the recordings and getting copyright clearances from people's managements and from copyright holders, that was a full-time job. However, Paul felt sure that NEMS could handle the paperwork. It was just a question of the recordings.

Our stoned discussions, which were sometimes held at John Dunbar's and Marianne Faithfull's flat at 29 Lennox Gardens in Knightsbridge, had led us into the fantasy world of a radio station, a television station and a newspaper. However, in the reality of daytime practicality we scaled down our ambitions a bit and decided that we could record the initial issues of the audio magazine ourselves and that later we could branch out into live recordings and extracts from BBC plays and so on which would all involve complex negotiations.

It would have made most sense to make an arrangement with Northern Songs, Lennon and McCartney's music publishers, to use their demo studios for the project, but we didn't think of that, or if we did the idea was probably rejected because we would be largely working in the evenings and night-time, whereas Denmark Street would be strictly daytime. I mentioned that my friend Ian Sommerville might be able to do the job of running a recording studio as he was the person who recorded the three spoken-word albums that I had produced earlier that summer: *Allen Ginsberg Reading at Better Books*, *Lawrence Ferlinghetti Reading at Better Books* and *Allen Ginsberg, Lawrence Ferlinghetti, Gregory Corso and Andrei Voznesensky Reading at the Architectural Association*. Earlier in the year Ian had recorded and produced William Burroughs's first album, *Call Me Burroughs*, in the *cave* beneath the English Bookshop in Paris and had been the technical brains behind the cut-up tapes that William Burroughs and Brion Gysin had been producing ever since 1960. Ian was gaunt, with sandy-brown hair that stood on end as he constantly ran his fingers through it in a nervous gesture. He had a degree in mathematics from Cambridge and was living in a hotel in Earls Court with William Burroughs, who had just returned to London after nine months in New York. Ian was also the man we employed to install the electrical wiring for the bookshop-gallery, so he had already met John Dunbar and Peter Asher.

A meeting was arranged at my flat to try to get the project started. I used the living-room as a painting studio, and the only lighting was

Miles and Peter Asher pose outside Indica Books' new premises at
102 Southampton Row for a feature in *16*, an American pop music magazine
(an edition of which can be seen in the window display)

John Dunbar looks down on his son Nicholas, who is playing on the steps leading to Indica's gallery from the bookshop. John, who was married to Marianne Faithfull, was a leading figure in the counterculture art movement. When Indica Gallery folded, he became an artist and collector.

a daylight fluorescent fitting that was uncomfortably bright for a meeting. However, Peter, Paul, Jane, Sue and I made ourselves comfortable as best we could, and everyone but Jane got high while Ian, for some reason, explained the principle of floating equations. Peter seemed interested, but it passed over the heads of the rest of us. Eventually we got him to calculate how much it would cost to equip a basic studio. Ian, still looking rather nervous, made a list: two Revox 736 tape-recorders, a pair of microphones with stands, amplifiers, speakers, a stock of tape, spare tape reels, a de-gauzer, editing block, blades, a cassette machine to make copies, a record player and various cables and bits and pieces. He wrote it all out in his beautiful copperplate writing along with an approximate costing of each and a total. He was expecting to discuss and justify each item – the Revoxes were about £150 each – but Paul gave the list a quick glance and returned it to Ian saying he should call Brian Epstein at a certain number and the payment would be taken care of. Done, just like that.

We still didn't know where this studio was to be located, but a day or two later Paul called in great excitement. Brian Epstein had bought an office building just one block from the Indica Gallery off Duke Street, St James's, and Paul had arranged with Brian that he, Peter, John Dunbar, Ian Sommerville and I were to have the top floor. The building came equipped with a fast modern lift, still a rarity in Britain. There was a reception room already furnished with a television and a carpet and an office where we could handle the paperwork, with a room leading off it that could house the studio. Paul was discussing plans for the studio with Epstein, as this was likely to be something rather more permanent than we had envisaged and would be used for auditions and as a demo studio for Brian's groups. It would need to be soundproofed and have mixing facilities, a lathe to make acetates and so on. Ian had estimated that it would cost about £9,000 to install all this.

Delighted by this turn of events, we calculated that the first issue of the magazine-album could be out in eight weeks. It was to have a long electronic piece by Paul that he had already recorded on his pair of Brenell tape-recorders, a 'mutter poem' by Pete Brown, who had performed a similar work by Kurt Schwitters that summer at the great Albert Hall poetry reading and who was now helping us construct and decorate Indica. There was to be a story by Adrian Mitchell, and Burroughs had promised a cut-up tape. We got as far as making a list of people who would receive free copies: Ginsberg, Ferlinghetti, Warhol, the Fugs, *East Village Other* and the other underground newspapers, before a problem over the office building occurred which meant that we had to put the project on hold.

Paul's solution was to install a temporary studio in an old flat that Ringo owned but no longer used because too many fans knew the address, while the new building was being fitted out. Paul rented it from him. It was in the ground floor and basement of 34 Montagu Square, not far from the Ashers' house on Wimpole Street where Peter and Paul lived and easy walking distance from my flat.

On a practical level, the studio was ideal for Ian because he was in a difficult position with his love life: he had been William Burroughs's boyfriend since the end of 1959, but at the end of 1964, when they were living in Tangier, Burroughs took off for New York, giving no indication when he was likely to return. He made various attempts to get Ian to join him but without success. After a few months Ian found a new boyfriend, Alan Watson, whom he met in his home town of Darlington while up there on a visit. Then Burroughs decided that he didn't like New York and returned to London where he moved into the Rushmore Hotel in Earls Court. Undecided what to do, Ian moved in with him. Then he moved Alan into a separate room in the Rushmore. Ian had no money, and Burroughs was paying for all of them. Not surprisingly there was a degree of tension. The situation was becoming farcical when the offer of Ringo's flat came up. It made sense for Ian actually to live there because it was in the evenings that people wanted to use the studio, and this would mean he

This photograph of John 'Hoppy' Hopkins was probably taken at Oxford in the early sixties. Hoppy began his photography career at *Melody Maker* magazine and photographed major bands from the Beatles to the Rolling Stones. He was a leading figure in the underground scene, founding cult venue the UFO Club, whose resident band was Pink Floyd, as well as the London Free School and co-founding *International Times* with Miles. He famously campaigned for the legalization of cannabis and was gaoled for six months; Paul McCartney secretly funded an advertisement in *The Times* in support of Hoppy. He became well known for his photography of CND marches and of peace events, as featured in *Peace News*. His work inspired so many of the events that form part of London's culture today, including the Notting Hill Carnival. He passed away on 30 January 2015. Hoppy's legacy lives on in his powerful photographs, which capture the true spirit of the sixties.

was always there. He and Alan moved in. It seemed a good way to compensate Ian for his time spent as a recording engineer. He could also make tape copies or record demos as a way of supplementing his income. Ian bought the equipment, all to studio quality and at a small discount from Teletape on Shaftesbury Avenue.

Now the studio existed, the problem arose of who was going to use it and who would produce the audio-magazine. In theory I would have been the best placed to edit the magazine because of my contacts in the literary world, but we were just starting Indica and my time was completely taken up with trying to get a rare book catalogue together, as well as simply getting the shop off the ground.

At the time I was also working with John Hopkins, 'Hoppy', on *Long Hair*, a literary magazine named by Allen Ginsberg that I edited and that Hoppy and I were printing and publishing ourselves. In addition, I still had some duties at Better Books as the new manager had not yet taken over. Paul obviously did not have the time to take an active role, nor did Peter. John was happy to use the studio to hang out and make recordings of his friends 'banging pots and pans', which at the time, with massive echo on them, did not sound at all bad but was also engaged in getting the Indica Gallery off the ground. Clearly we should have appointed an editor to do the work, but Paul did not want to employ anyone – it was supposed to be a relaxed, spontaneous, underground project, and as soon as anyone got employed, like it or not, it was a business.

We were hoping that people would get to hear of the project and somehow produce the tapes themselves, but of course the studio had an unlisted phone number, and as the flat still belonged to Ringo he didn't want the address given out. Ian regarded it as Paul's studio, Paul thought of it as some kind of 'people's studio', but with no one in charge it sat there unused except for social purposes. Paul, John Dunbar, Peter, Sue and I often met there of an evening, with Ian and Alan playing the role of hosts, fixing everyone drinks and snacks – Alan worked as a chef in, of all places, Scotland Yard. Ian was particularly worried about Ringo's green watered-silk wallpaper as it was easily marked. Paul would often bring over acetates from the tracks of *Revolver* that the Beatles were working on, and it became a very convivial little scene, like a private club. Paul was still living in the Asher household, and although he had friends over he couldn't easily hold court in Mrs Asher's living-room.

William Burroughs was still seeing Ian Sommerville and he became one of the first people to use the studio, recording a series of stereo experiments there as well as many hours of tape cut-ups. He and Ian had previously been involved in several experimental films directed by Antony Balch: *Towers Open Fire* and *Cut Ups*, as well as making hundreds of hours of cut-up tapes together. Sadly none of his tapes from that period still exist. Paul was one of the other people to use the studio and soon got to know Burroughs. They discussed ideas associated with cut-ups and random juxta-positions; Paul had often noticed how well any randomly selected piece of music would go with one of the experimental silent films that he was making at that time. The brain seemed to find corre-spondences and link them together. Paul's films were usually com-posed of two separate takes, one superimposed over the other in a completely random way. Burroughs was still engaged in making cut-up texts as well as collage scrapbooks, film experiments with Balch and actual cut-up tapes. It was Paul's friendship with Burroughs, and their conversations at the studio, that led him to put Burroughs on the sleeve of *Sgt Pepper* in 1967. Paul recalled his times with Burroughs in the studio:

> In our conversations, I thought about getting into cut-ups and things like that and I thought I would use it [the studio] for cut-ups, so I kind of thought I might do that. But I think it ended up being of more practical use to me, really, [to] let Burroughs

Top: At Allen Ginsberg's thirty-ninth birthday party in London on 3 June 1965. Chatting are, left to right, Barry Miles, Allen Ginsberg and Ian Sommerville. Later on at the party Allen stripped naked and was wearing his pants on his head when John Lennon and George Harrison arrived with their wives; they didn't stay long.

Bottom: William Burroughs in Paris, 1964. This picture is taken from the film

do the cut-ups and let me just go in and demo things. So I'd just written 'Eleanor Rigby' and I just went down there in the basement in a day off on my own. Just took a guitar down. I'm not sure there was anyone there. I just operated the little Revox and just used it as a demo studio. But occasionally Burroughs would be there. He was very interesting, he was fine, but the sitting around for hours would be more with Ian Sommerville and his friend, Alan. I remember them telling me off for being a teahead. 'You're a teahead, man!' 'Well? So?'[3]

This was a bit much, coming from Ian who was constantly stoned and had been for many years. In any case, it was not meant as a rebuke. One of Ian's fondest memories of his time in Tangier with Burroughs was that his pillow had been stuffed with marijuana: 'Gives you great dreams, man!' Burroughs, a man of relatively few words unless drunk or stoned, was happy to sit and watch while McCartney worked. He was intrigued to watch the development of 'Eleanor Rigby', which began as a simple acoustic track with Paul strumming his guitar, most of the time using Ian as his tape op, and was worked up to a stage where Paul knew exactly how he wanted the arrangement to go.

Eventually Paul abandoned the experimental studio as unworkable. It had to be used for something more than banging pots and rubbing the rims of wine glasses and clearly was not going to be. After a couple of months Ian moved out, taking the equipment with him with Paul's agreement. Years later someone turned up to take away one of the Revoxes. Paul gave the remaining tape-recorders and the rest of the equipment to Ian. The idea of the experimental studio and the magazine, however, remained in his head, and almost three years later it surfaced again in the form of the experimental division of Apple Records: Zapple.

Our stoned discussions, which were
sometimes held at John Dunbar's
and Marianne Faithfull's flat at
29 Lennox Gardens in Knightsbridge,
had led us into the fantasy world
of a radio station, a television
station and a newspaper.

Chapter 2

The Idea

Yoko Ono demonstrating her ceiling installation at her show at Indica Gallery.
Viewers had to climb the stepladder and use a magnifying glass to read a tiny text
on the panel. Lennon climbed up on the day he met her.

The Idea

LESS THAN A YEAR after we opened, Indica Books moved to its own premises near the British Museum in Bloomsbury. The gallery was in the appropriate location, but the bookshop wasn't. There was no passing trade, and although we were doing our best to publicize ourselves with pictures and interviews in magazines most people had no idea that Indica Books existed. We decided to separate the bookshop from the art gallery, and fortuitously, in the summer of 1966, John Dunbar met Chris Hill who had somehow acquired a bookshop called Jackson's at 102 Southampton Row, one block from the British Museum in Bloomsbury. A complicated deal was done in which Chris became a director of Indica and also received a cash sum in order for us to take over his premises. The money, inevitably, came from Paul McCartney. Chris and his younger twin brothers, Jeffrey and Alan, lived above the shop at 18 Ormonde Mansions, 106 Southampton Row, and were frequently in the shop. It was through his involvement with Indica that Chris met Denny Laine, who had been the lead singer with the Moody Blues – he sang on 'Go Now', their biggest hit – and worked on a number of musical projects with him. We installed a huge noticeboard, which was quickly covered with notices of readings, items for sale and personal messages. William Burroughs appealed for volunteers for him to practise Scientology auditing and even gave out his telephone number – rare for him; Yoko Ono appealed for babysitters – we had to take this down in the end because several people complained that they had babysat until the early hours for her and she never paid them; musicians wanted to form bands; bands wanted musicians. There was a big brown teapot, and tea was offered (this was before the ubiquitous coffee in bookshops), and the big room in the back was used initially for overflow exhibitions from the gallery, the first show being the Baschet Brothers' sculpture-instruments.

In October 1966 *International Times* (usually known as *IT*), Europe's first underground newspaper, began publishing from the big room in the basement. I was a director and also contributed a regular literary column, as well as a record review column. Our music coverage increased when one day I complained to Paul McCartney that we were finding it difficult to get advertising and he suggested the obvious: 'Why don't you interview me for the paper, then you'll get record company advertising?' He was right, of course. I went over to his place and recorded a conversation with him which we ran as a Q&A in the fifth issue of the paper. After that record company advertising became a major source of income for the paper. Paul suggested that I interview 'my friend George', so I invited George over to my flat for tea and recorded a tape with him. After that it was easy. Mick Jagger came to tea, and I taped him, he was followed by Pete Townshend and others. I never had to go through record companies or publicists; it was all done on a friendly basis because the musicians knew *IT* and liked it and wanted to be in it and support it.

There is no question that without Paul McCartney's support Indica Books would have gone under several years before it did (it closed on 29 February 1970). Paul was a good friend and supporter of the underground scene, although of necessity he kept his involvement quiet. Years later Paul talked about this period of his life:

> When John was living out in the suburbs by the golf course with Cynthia and hanging out there, I was getting in with a guy called Miles and the people at Indica. I used to be at his house a lot of nights, just him and his wife, because he was just so interesting, very well read. So he'd turn you on to Burroughs

ALL NIGHT RAVE to launch
new underground newspaper
'INTERNATIONAL TIMES' it
the Soft Machine ; the Pink Floyd ;
steel bands
STRIP - TRIPS - HAPPENING
MOVIE - POP - OP - COSTUME
MASQUE - DRAG BALL
bring your own poison, bring
Flowers & Gass filled balloons
SurPRIZE for shortest & Barest
at...
THE ROUND HOUSE *
opp. chalk farm underground
SAT. 15th OCT 11 P.M. onwards
advance tickets 5/- from INDICA
better books ; Dobells Record Shop.
GRANNIE TAKE A TRIP
Mandarin Book Shops at...
Nottinghill gate & Swiss
Cottage, or compulsory
donations of 10/- at door.

The launch of *International Times* has been described as one of the important moments in the sixties counterculture revolution. The launch, held at the Roundhouse (this was its first public event), featured Pink Floyd, among many other avant-garde artists. *IT* embodied the free-thinking and cutting-edge arts movement of the sixties and flew the flag for London's underground scene

The International Times   No. 6   Jan 16-29, 1967 / 1s.

★**Paul McCARTNEY**
★**Norman MAILER**
★**William BURROUGHS**
★**Allen GINSBERG**
★**Cerebral CORTEX**

Above: Paul was a great supporter of *International Times*, not only raising its profile by agreeing to be interviewed but also often dipping into his own pocket to keep the paper afloat. This cover was kindly donated by *IT* art director, Mike McInnerney.

Overleaf: Peter Asher and Miles at the till in Indica Books, April 1967. The first cash till for the shop was donated by Jane Asher and was the same Victorian till she used when playing 'shops' as a little girl.

and all that. I'd done a bit of literature at school, but I never really did anything modern. I find this very interesting because it's something I realize I didn't put around a lot at the time, like I helped start *International Times* with Miles, helped start Indica Bookshop and Gallery, where John met Yoko.[1]

Indica Gallery closed in 1967, but the bookshop struggled on. It was in late September 1968 that I went to see Paul McCartney at his house on Cavendish Avenue in St John's Wood. Indica Books was once more in trouble financially, and as Paul had always said to come to him if we needed further help I was doing so, albeit with trepidation. I didn't like asking for money because I thought it affected our friendship and I was also the one who approached him for help whenever *International Times* needed money to pay the staff; too many of the people he knew were hitting on him. However, he did say that I should never be scared to come to him if things were really bad. 'Years from now,' he said, 'twenty years from now', and it did look as if Indica Books would fold without an injection of cash, so I went begging once more. At least it was for the bookshop, not for me. I gave the secret three long rings on the doorbell, which all the girls gathered by the black metal gate knew anyway – they had eyes and ears – and was admitted. Paul's house was set back from the road, with a front yard serving as a driveway. To the left of the house was the garage, concealing his Aston Martin DB5 and his wide-wheelbase black-glass Mini Cooper. The yard was lit by a Victorian street lamp, installed by Paul. Tea was served in his living-room, and we sat there like two English gentlemen. I asked for £3,000, to which he readily agreed and then quickly changed the subject, as if he were as embarrassed as I was at bringing it up.

Paul, having split up with Jane, was in what he later described as his 'bachelor period', and the house was full of semi-clad young women, one of whom looked in on us. Paul told her to go away; that

we were talking business. She pulled a face and left. 'It's terrible,' he said. 'The birds are always quarrelling about something. There's three living here at the moment.' He laughed, because this was quite a new departure for him. Mostly I'd only ever visited the house when Jane Asher was there. 'And there's another one, an American groupie, flying in this evening. I've thrown her out once. I had to throw her suitcase over the wall. But it's no good; she keeps coming back.'

Paul was clearly very pleased about something, and, business over, he leaped up and led the way upstairs to his music room. 'Come and hear this,' he said. He put on a white label acetate of 'Back in the USSR' that he had finished mixing the night before. 'How do you think the cocky Americans will like that?' he asked, and we both laughed.

In fact there was further business to discuss. Just a few weeks before we had been talking once more about a series of very cheap spoken-word albums, issued regularly if possible, like a magazine. Paul saw this as a way of involving me, and also Indica Books, with Apple and had asked me to prepare a list of people I thought that Apple should record. I had the list with me and showed it to him. In no particular order it comprised the following poets and writers: an initial group to include Allen Ginsberg, William S. Burroughs, Richard Brautigan, Lawrence Ferlinghetti, Henry Miller, Kenneth Patchen, Michael McClure, Ken Weaver, Ed Sanders, Charles Olson and Charles Bukowski; I didn't expect them all to happen. This would be followed by Anaïs Nin, Robert Creeley, Ed Dorn, Samuel Beckett, Gary Snyder, Simon Vinkenoog, Tom Pickard and I even thought of approaching Ezra Pound to read his *Confucian Analects*.

Almost all of the people on my first list lived in the USA, and Paul thought it would be better to start with people who might be known there, if only by a small number of people. Paul had met both Ginsberg and Burroughs, and certainly knew of Miller, but the rest I suspected he had never heard of. None the less his response was

Paul at Cavendish Avenue, during his 'bachelor phase' after splitting up with long-term girlfriend Jane Asher. Paul met his future wife, Linda Eastman, in 1967, and they met again in 1968 when he and John Lennon went to New York to announce the launch of Apple Records. Paul and Linda were married on 12 March 1969.

Top: The participating poets in the International Poetry Incarnation line-up before the event in front of the Albert Memorial, Kensington. From left to right are: Barbara Rubin, Harry Fainlight, Adrian Mitchell, Alexander Trocchi, Anselm Hollo, Marcus Field, Allen Ginsberg, Michael Horovitz, John Esam, Ernst Jandl and Dan Richter.

Bottom: Lawrence Ferlinghetti interviews Allen Ginsberg in front of the Shakespeare statue at the Albert Memorial, Kensington, during a press conference for the International Poetry Incarnation. The event, held on 11 June 1965, was inspired by Allen Ginsberg's reading at Better Books, then managed by Miles. Over 7,000 people attended the readings at the Royal Albert Hall, marking a definitive moment in the avant-garde movement.

enthusiastic. 'Great,' he said. 'Terrific. Get it together! Get an assistant and go out there and record them. Done. Just like that!' He laughed. I laughed.

I had followed the course of Apple from its first inception as a place where creative people could get funding. It had been discussed at my flat, and I had sat in on long discussions about the project at John Dunbar's flat and at Paul's house. Now he explained that they were thinking of launching a separate label on which to release more obscure material, because anything like that on Apple would be swamped by the Beatles and their more commercial acts. I thought this was a good idea.

Back in June 1968 an Apple internal memo had been circulated to 'everyone' which read, 'Try to think of suggestions for a subsidiary label for Apple, which would put out more freaky sounds.' In the end the name for the new label came from John Lennon who said, 'A is for Apple, Z is for Zapple.' The name had nothing to do with Frank Zappa, who was, however, miffed by the use of, as he saw it, his name. He was particularly irritated because Zapple appeared to be doing the same thing that he was doing with his Bizarre and Straight labels: in 1968 he released albums by Lenny Bruce and by Wild Man Fischer, both of which could be seen as anthropological studies of the late sixties culture. Zapple had also announced that they were going to release some Lord Buckley and Lenny Bruce tapes, so Zappa saw it as a commercial rival. John Lennon, however, was not interested in youth culture; his concern was with anthropological recordings of his own life with Yoko, beginning with *Two Virgins*, which he considered so important that the world should know all about it; therefore to have a dedicated label was a perfect solution for him.

This was a time when travel was difficult and very expensive; a ticket to New York cost three months' salary. People listened to far more spoken-word and documentary records back then, particularly of recordings made in foreign locations. We often sat around listening to a Folkways album called *New York 19* from 1954, compiled by sound archivist Tony Schwartz, which consisted of nothing but snippets of street sounds and short excerpts from ethnic music or religious ceremonies. One track was a brief interview with a road worker who was digging a hole in the road with a pneumatic drill. 'I lost a quarter here two days ago, and I'm looking for it', he told the interviewer. I had another album of a ceremony in a Japanese Zen monastery. One friend had an entire album about Eskimos, including several tracks where all that could be heard was a fisherman scraping a hole in the ice. These were commercial recordings: in the fifties there had been several best-selling albums demonstrating stereo with recordings of table-tennis games; Elvis sold masses of copies of *Elvis Sails*, a spoken-word EP from March 1959 consisting of nothing but his press conferences, and in 1970 *Songs of the Humpback Whale* was a best-seller. Parlophone, the Beatles' own label at EMI, specialized in comedy and spoken-word albums. Seen in this light, the concept of releasing albums filled with poetry, conversations and fragments was not such a far-out idea.

There were a number of meetings, many with Peter Asher who was the head of A&R at Apple and so, technically, my boss. Mostly though, we sat around at my place or Paul's discussing what could be released. I was very satisfied with how the spoken-word recording I made of Allen Ginsberg, Lawrence Ferlinghetti, Gregory Corso and Andrei Voznesensky reading at the Architectural Association had come out. It was everything that the Royal Albert Hall reading a few weeks earlier had not been: the poets were on form, they read well, they chose easily accessible works and were very well received. The record caught the atmosphere well. At Zapple we planned to record a series of live poetry readings, each featuring five or six poets: the 'Liverpool Scene' poets – Adrian Henri, Brian Patten, Roger McGough; the New York Poetry Project poets at St Mark's

Church in New York – Ann Waldman, Ted Berrigan, Ron Padgett; and the poets and writers surrounding City Lights Books in San Francisco. Paul was keen on the idea of a record of William Burroughs talking about different drugs as well as reading from his work, and he also wanted to release BBC radio plays such as its production of *Ubu Cocu* by Alfred Jarry that he had listened to on his car radio while driving to Liverpool one time and which he had enjoyed very much. He thought it would be good to have such a performance readily available. We talked about setting up a deal with the BBC for a separate series of such recordings. None of it would have cost very much money compared to many of the other Apple projects.

On 3 October I had written to all the Americans on my list and had already taken a tentative step forward on the Michael McClure album. McClure was a poet and playwright, the author of *Dark Brown, Billy the Kid, The Beard* (which was performed in London in November 1968 to great acclaim) and many other titles. I had heard a tape from 1964 of him roaring his 'Beast Language' poems at the lions in the Fleishaker Zoo in San Francisco and of them roaring back at him, recorded one morning before the zoo opened by Bruce Connor. This sounded like our sort of thing, and so I obtained a copy of the tape from him, and the first actual studio activity on the Zapple label was to remaster Connor's tape on to 15 inches per second (ips) at Abbey Road.

Paul, Peter and I discussed the idea of getting politicians to explain their political positions. We thought that the real motivation and reasoning behind much of the news was lost, or certainly misunderstood, and felt that people, particularly young people and Beatles fans, would benefit from hearing why leaders such as Castro or Mao made the decisions that they did. Consequently big boxes of Beatles records were sent out to Fidel Castro, Mao Tse Tung, Indira Gandhi and others, together with requests to record an interview for us or to allow us to record them. None of them responded, and it is unlikely that the records ever reached their intended recipients.

One of the most innovative ideas for the time was simply to record the Beatles discussing their upcoming album, complete with a few false starts to tracks or some rehearsals – the Beatles often blasted their way through some golden oldies in order to warm up before a session began. Paul thought that this was a great plan because it was publicity for their albums. It prefigured the idea of journalists releasing their interview tapes as albums, the first of which was *The Beatles Tapes* in 1976. The first recordings of out-takes and rehearsals were released six months later when the first rock bootleg, *Great White Wonder* by Bob Dylan, was released. It was this concept that *anything* could be recorded and released that was so great, and around the Christmas 1968 period everyone seemed enthusiastic about the idea.

Back in June 1968 an Apple internal memo had been circulated to 'everyone' which read: 'Try to think of suggestions for a subsidiary label for Apple, which would put out more freaky sounds.' In the end, the name for the new label came from John Lennon who said, 'A is

Chapter 3

Savile Row

Once this door opened on to the business empire of the Beatles – the Apple offices at 3 Savile Row, London. The building would become the site for their famous rooftop concert. Fans still visit the landmark, many leaving behind their own tribute to the boys.

Savile Row

APPLE WAS NOW A fully functioning record label, although already some of its initial idealism and adventurous spirit was being sorely tested. On 20 April 1968 Apple had placed advertisements in the UK and the USA advertising for talent using a photograph of Alistair Taylor posing as a one-man band, saying, 'This man now owns a Bentley.' This was followed up in May by a trip to New York and John and Paul going on the *Today Show* on 15 May to announce Apple and to appeal for film scripts and cassettes. Johnny Carson was on holiday, so they were interviewed by regular stand-in Joe Garagiola, a former baseball catcher, who appeared to know little about the Beatles. The interview was further disrupted by an apparently inebriated Tallulah Bankhead who kept interrupting. But John and Paul were veteran interviewees and managed to get their point across.

Joe G: Could you tell us about your newest corporate business venture?

John: It's a business concerning records, films and electronics and, as a sideline, manufacturing or whatever. We want to set up a system whereby people who just want to make a film about anything don't have to go on their knees in somebody's office, probably yours.

Paul: We really want to help people but without doing it like a charity or seeming like ordinary patrons of the arts. I mean, we're in the happy position of not really needing any more money, so for the first time the bosses aren't in it for the profit. If you come and see me and say, 'I've had such and such a dream', I will say, 'Here's so much money. Go away and do it.'

We've already bought all our dreams, so now we want to share that possibility with others. There's no desire in any of our heads to take over the world. That was Hitler. There is, however, a desire to get power in order to use it for good.

John: The aim of this company isn't really a stack of gold teeth in the bank. We've done that bit. It's more of a trick to see if we can actually get artistic freedom within a business structure, to see if we can create nice things and sell them without charging three times our cost.

Joe G: How will you run your new company?

John: There's people we can get to do that. We don't know anything about business.

Naturally they were inundated. Denis O'Dell had to hire five people just to read through the film scripts that Apple Films received, and, after they moved to Savile Row, a room off Derek Taylor's press office was designated 'the Black Hole' where sackloads of cassettes were stored, never to be listened to. They received hundreds of poetry manuscripts, even though book publishing was not one of their announced areas of activity. The first person to apply for money in Britain was Yoko Ono, who asked for £5,000 to make a film (this was before she and John got together). Her project was rejected.

On 5 May Twiggy saw Mary Hopkin on *Opportunity Knocks*, a television talent show, and telephoned Paul to say that he really should sign her to Apple. On 11 August Apple Records was launched. On 16 August Mary Hopkin's 'Those Were the Days' was released, produced by Paul McCartney. It went to number one.

On 22 June 1968 Apple paid half a million pounds to bandleader Jack Hylton for 3 Savile Row, a large Georgian townhouse built in 1733 just off Regent Street in the West End, which had previously been the Albany Club (Albany, a private residential street, was just across the road). The door was guarded by Jimmy Clarke in his uniform of a dove-grey morning coat, a high, stiff collar and tight black trousers, as if he were the maître d' at the Ritz. He was friendly but firm; however, a fair number of fans did manage to sneak in while he was distracted or doing other business. Inside, in the large entrance hall, the walls were all white, the telephones were all white and the deep pile carpet was apple green. At the end was the main staircase, with a subsidiary one to the left; there was plaster panelling in all the main rooms, including the entrance hall, dados, entablatures, cornices and in the back room on the ground floor was a row of columns. To the right of the stairs was the reception and Debbie, the receptionist; a few gold records on the wall, a row of chairs, the music magazines and trade press, with doors leading to Ron Kass's office and the big back room. As head of the record division Ron had more visitors than anyone except the press office. Displayed on the main staircase was an oil painting of two lion cubs; otherwise the walls were lined with gold records. On the first floor in the building's two principal rooms were the offices of Neil Aspinall and Peter Brown. The front room ran the full width of the building and featured elaborate plaster moulding on the ceiling.[1]

Derek Taylor's press office was on the third floor. It was a large room, dominated by Derek's high scallop-backed white wicker chair that he had shipped from Los Angeles when he moved to London to join the Beatles. It was known as the 'throne of Apple', and it was from here that he managed to keep in check the waves of madness caused by John and Paul inviting every nutter, crazy, hustler and conman in the Western world to apply to them for funds. It was also the public face of the Beatles. All the celebrities visiting London from the USA or Europe wanted to drop in on Apple, it was one of the sights: Jane Fonda, Lauren Bacall, Harry Nilsson, Duane Eddy, Dennis Hopper. It was always fun to stroll in and share a glass of wine with Michelle Phillips from the Mamas and the Papas. Being in the front line was an exhausting business, and Derek was fortified

At Apple. Standing, from left to right, are Denis O'Dell, Paul McCartney, 'Magic Alex', Brian Lewis (O'Dell's assistant), Ron Kass; seated to the right of the desk is Neil Aspinall and, in front, John Lennon with Derek Taylor.

Apple have moved house from 95, Wigmore St., to 3, Savile Row, London W1. Telephone 734/8232

Top: The moving card sent out from Apple to announce their new offices. This card was sent to all their contacts prior to the opening of the 3 Savile Row offices in July 1968. This card was bought directly from Apple Scruff Lizzie Bravo, who, in February 1968, was one of two Beatles fans recruited by Paul McCartney outside the EMI Abbey Road Studios to provide backing vocals on 'Across the Universe'.

Bottom: A matchbook from the Apple offices featuring the logo on the front and address on the back; visitors to the Apple offices were given an array of such tokens. Both items are courtesy of the Mark Naboshek Collection.

by frequent joints and drinks, although he was asked early on to stop taking LSD during the working day.

To keep the world informed of the Beatles' moves and plans and to deal with the madness of the American press during the absurd days of the 'Paul is dead' fiasco required a number of assistants, the main ones being Mavis Smith, ex-Ballet Rambert dancer and married to the editor of *Melody Maker*, and Carol Paddon, who came to him from Terry Doran and whose desk was next to the toy birds – they endlessly dipped their beaks into a tray filled with water and were irritatingly fascinating. Richard DiLello, the 'House Hippie' rolled joints, ran errands, poured drinks, pasted cuttings into books and made himself useful. There were more typists and a series of other young men and women who drifted in and found themselves working there for weeks, often without pay. Chris O'Dell, the woman 'from Tucson Arizona', was one of these. She was a close friend of Derek Taylor from Los Angeles, and after doing odd jobs such as filing press cuttings, getting in the lunches and relieving Laurie at the switchboard she was finally given a job as Peter Asher's personal assistant.

Peter was initially next door to the press office, but there were too many interruptions there, so he moved to the top floor of the building, the fifth, up in the eaves. It was quieter up there and he could get on with his work of listening to tapes. Peter had put his faith in James Taylor, a young American songwriter, and was hard at work producing his first album. Peter had so much faith that James was even staying with him at his flat on Weymouth Street. When Allen Klein took over Apple Peter left, taking James with him. Peter managed him and produced *Sweet Baby James*, Taylor's first massive hit album.

Chris had a small room next to Peter's office furnished with a purple desk, taken from the ill-fated Apple Boutique, and a cane rocking-chair from Derek's press office.

At first Paul was the only Beatle to make regular appearances at Apple. He came in most days and was concerned at the amount of money haemorrhaging from the building. Directors were treating themselves to the finest wines over luncheon, everyone travelled first class; the entertainment and travel bills were enormous. Unfortunately it was the press office who bore the brunt of Paul's criticism. It was the most obviously visible example of money being wasted as far as he could see. But they were only doing their job, which was to represent the Beatles. Far from having to publicize 'the boys', their job was to fend off the press, placate and stroke the reporters and try, on the side, to promote the other artists that Apple had signed. Paul's and John's appearance on television offering to help anyone who needed money for a project had resulted in an endless stream of people, all demanding attention. Some were satisfied with a drink or a joint or some free records, some received a small amount of money, and others had to be escorted, swearing, from the building. The Beatles started it, and some-one had to deal with it. Paul's attempts to cut back on expenses met with obstruction, not from the staff but from the other Beatles:

> I'd say, 'Let's not booze all day'; 'Let's not employ millions of chicks in mini-skirts even though it does look nice, and they smell nice and those angora sweaters are rather dishy, but let's not do all that.' I'm referring to the press office. I once tried to get rid of one of the secretaries, but she was a bit comely and they all threatened to resign. Derek Taylor threatened to resign and I said, 'Well?' I was trying to hold my own. Then George came in and saw me. 'She goes . . .' [Paul imitates a pleading look.] 'We all go . . .' [Paul spreads hands in despairing gesture. The secretary stayed on.] 'Ooops!' Actually what I was trying to do was slim down the rather overloaded press department where there were a few nice chicks and a lot of booze, and, as you say, you used to go there, so did everyone else. That was the place to go.[2]

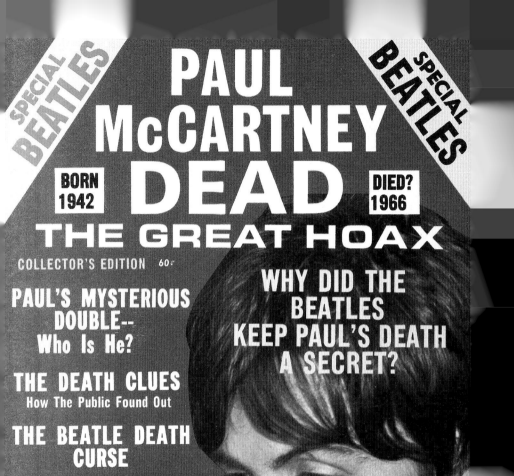

SPECIAL BEATLES

PAUL McCARTNEY DEAD

BORN 1942

DIED? 1966

THE GREAT HOAX

COLLECTOR'S EDITION 60¢

**PAUL'S MYSTERIOUS DOUBLE--
Who Is He?**

THE DEATH CLUES
How The Public Found Out

THE BEATLE DEATH CURSE

WHY DID THE BEATLES KEEP PAUL'S DEATH A SECRET?

When the world went mad over the supposed death of Paul McCartney. In September–October 1969 rumours that Paul McCartney had died and that the Beatles had covered it up began to spread like wildfire across the world. Fans analysed records and album covers endlessly for clues substantiating the theory. Finally Paul, who had been living quietly in Scotland with his family, did an in-depth interview with *Life* magazine to quell the rumours, although conspiracy theorists continued to speculate. This special edition *Paul McCartney Dead: The Great Hoax* magazine was published in the USA in late 1969 by Country Wide Publications, New York City. Courtesy of the Mark Naboshek Collection.

The consumption of drink in the press office was listed by Chris O'Dell in her memoir *Miss O'Dell*. In one two-week period they consumed eight bottles of J&B Scotch, four bottles of Courvoisier, three bottles of vodka, forty-eight lagers, ninety-six Coca-Colas, twenty-four ginger ales, twenty-four bitter lemons, twelve tonic waters, twelve tomato juices, thirty-six bottles of lime juice and six hundred cigarettes. There was also a fairly large block of hash that was not on her list. In fact the press office expenses cost nothing in comparison to even one trip by one of the directors: first class to New York, best hotel, expensive dining with the finest wines for a group of record business executives. None the less, Paul began making lists of who did what, intending to cut out some of the dead wood.

There were vague attempts made to cut back on spending. Instead of the expensive restaurant bills, they hired Penny, a Cordon Bleu cook, so that the Beatles and the directors could eat in. Few of the staff utilized her culinary skills: Lennon wanted jam butties, Ringo wanted 'soldiers' (buttered toast cut in strips with the crusts cut off) that he dipped into soft boiled eggs and ate with a cup of tea, George sometimes called for a cup of Earl Grey from Fortnum's but usually went for an omelette and chips at lunch. Penny sometimes knocked out a soufflé for them, but they would call down later and say they were still hungry so could she send up some chips. She was wasted on them, but other members of staff quickly realized what was on offer and sent up their requests. However, as far as business was concerned, everything seemed to be going well: 'Hey Jude', the first Beatles record released on their own label, went to number one. Then, on 18 October, John and Yoko were busted.

Paul's and John's appearance on television offering to help anyone who needed money for a project had resulted in an endless stream of people, all demanding attention. Some were satisfied with a drink or a joint or some free records, some received a small amount of money, and others had to be escorted, swearing, from the building.

Chapter 4

Blue Meanies

John and Yoko, leaving court surrounded by police in 19 October 1968 after John's hearing for possession of drugs. The hearing lasted only five minutes with bail being granted. However, when they left Marylebone Magistrates' Court they realized that their car was not ready to pick them up, and John tried to shield the pregnant Yoko from the scrum of press, who were outside waiting for them.

Blue Meanies

JOHN AND YOKO WERE living in Ringo's old flat in Montagu Square, where Paul's experimental studio had been located a few years before. They had advance warning; the police usually tipped off Fleet Street if a celebrity bust was coming up so they could send a reporter and photographer (a service that was of course paid for, but clearly neither the press nor the police were going to complain about it). Don Short, the showbusiness correspondent from the *Daily Mirror*, called John and told him what was coming up. Cleaning flats was not something that John and Yoko did, so John had imperiously called his old school friend Pete Shotton and asked him to do it. This was not the first time it had happened. As Tony Bramwell, Apple employee and a friend of Lennon's and Shotton's since the early days in Liverpool, recalled, 'Pete went reluctantly because his feelings had been deeply wounded by the arrogant way John and Yoko treated him, calling upon him to clean up the pigsty of an apartment when the mess got too much for them. The final straw came when he was expected to do Yoko's laundry. He had said to John, "John, it's me, Pete – remember?" before storming off. Nevertheless, he was there when John needed him. They'd gone through the flat like a whirlwind, getting rid of the traces of every drug. Pete was carrying out piles of trash when Yoko turned up. "Get rid of him!" she screamed to John.'[1] Pete felt that he would have probably found the small stashes of cannabis that Pilcher's sniffer dog, Willy, discovered, but it did not matter much whether the pot was all found and disposed of because Pilcher was well known to always bring his own, just in case. In fact he later spent time in gaol for planting evidence.

Detective Sergeant Pilcher and his gang of heavies found 219 grains of cannabis. In court Mr Frisby for the prosecution said a cigarette rolling machine was found on top of a bathroom mirror, a film canister and a cigarette case were found in the bedroom and were said to contain traces of cannabis resin. The police found 27.3 grains of cannabis in an envelope in a suitcase, and 19.8 grains were found in a binocular case nosed out by a police sniffer dog. On 28 November 1968 Lennon, who pleaded guilty of sole possession, was fined £150 with 20 guineas of costs at Marylebone Magistrates' Court. It was to be the cause of the years of problems that Lennon went on to have with the American immigration authorities. It was fortunate that heroin was not found or else his problems in the USA might have been significantly worse.

John downplayed his addiction in an interview with *Rolling Stone*, saying, 'I never injected it or anything. We sniffed a little when we were in real pain. We got such a hard time from everyone, and I've had so much thrown at me, and at Yoko, especially at Yoko . . . We took "H" because of what the Beatles and others were doing to us. But we got out of it.'[2] Of course it doesn't matter how you take it, you are still an addict. As William Burroughs memorably said, 'You can shoot it, sniff it or shove it up your ass, it doesn't matter. It's still junk and you're still a junkie.'[3]

John's and Yoko's heroin addiction presented a number of problems because, like most junkies, they were very manipulative. John wanted his way on which tracks of his were to appear on the *White Album* and was prepared to do deals in order to achieve what he wanted. He told *Rolling Stones*'s Jann Wenner:

I did a job on this banker that we were using, and on a few other people, and on the Beatles . . . How do you describe the job? You know, you know, my job – I maneuver people. That's what leaders do, and I sit and make situations, which will be of benefit to me with other people, it's as simple as that. I had to do a job to get Allen [Klein] in Apple. I did a job, so did Yoko

. . . Maneuvering is what it is, let's not be coy about it. It is a deliberate and thought-out maneuver of how to get a situation the way we want it. That's how life's about, isn't it, is it not?

This attitude extended into John's, and through John, into Yoko's way of dealing with Apple. They used it largely as a vehicle for their own ideas and projects and had little interest in the other Apple divisions or the success of other Apple artists.

John and Yoko brought Allen Klein in. Klein began as an accountant. He was famous for finding errors in royalty statements. Klein had some history with the Beatles. In 1964, when he was managing Sam Cooke, he had a meeting with Brian Epstein and said that he had heard that the Beatles' royalty rates from EMI were 'for shit'. He told Brian he could get them a million pounds if Brian would let him renegotiate their contract and take a fee. As Peter Brown reported, 'Brian was royally offended . . . and he had Klein shown to the door'.[4] The story of how Klein managed to reach John Lennon is long and complicated, but once he got John and Yoko into his suite at the Dorchester he put on such a convincing act that at the end of the evening Lennon wrote a note to Sir Joseph Lockwood, head of EMI Records, saying, 'From now on Allen Klein handles all my stuff.'

After the arrival of Allen Klein, John and Yoko began to use Apple as their personal fiefdom. In his memoir Tony Bramwell wrote, 'From the day Yoko went official as John's lover, she had another desk and chair moved into his office and started taking over, laying down the law, issuing orders. I have never seen anyone so assured, so completely in control, so much a pain in the ass.'[5] By now the Beatles were working on the *White Album*, but John insisted that Yoko be with him at all times. She sat next to him on the piano stool and sometimes made musical suggestions, much to the repressed fury of the other three Beatles who would never have allowed their partners to make anything other than the occasional visit to a recording session. From time to time John and Yoko would go off to the toilets together. The other Beatles were astonished that John even wanted her with him when he went for a piss, but of course they were going to snort a line of heroin. When Yoko was recovering from her miscarriage a bed was moved into Abbey Road where they were recording the *White Album* and a microphone suspended above her head in case she wanted to make any comments.

John railed to anyone who would listen that the other Beatles and the staff of Apple hated Yoko because they were racists, but this was not true. As Derek Taylor pointed out, they didn't hate her, but they didn't love her either. As for the accusation of racism – musicians and most of the music industry have traditionally always been free of racism and bigotry, although there might have been a residual anti-Japanese feeling (the war had only ended twenty years earlier and stories about Japanese wartime atrocities frequently featured in the newspapers). Still, the real reason that people disliked Yoko was because she ordered them about and sent them on errands in a particularly rude way; she was brought up with servants, and that's how she treated the staff of Apple. George found it particularly galling that she never gave the Beatles their definite article. He told me, 'She would say, "Beatles do this" and "Beatles do that", and we would say, "Uh, it's the Beatles actually, love." She'd look at you and say, "Beatles do this."' And he laughed and shrugged his shoulders. Whether Yoko was ever aware of the disruption her presence caused to the Beatles' working practices I don't know. Some people thought she was so involved in her own work and self-interest that she didn't notice; others thought that it was a deliberate ploy to separate John off from the others.

The album took from the end of May to the middle of October 1968 to record, and although fraught with difficulties – both George and Ringo walked out at different points – the tension didn't seem to worry Lennon who contributed some magnificent songs to it

John Lennon with his Rickenbacker at a recording session at Teddington Studios.
John was the band's rhythm guitarist, influenced by the Everly Brothers and
Ray Charles (at his most melodic). Lennon had a real affinity for Rickenbacker
guitars; he bought his first one – a Capri 325 – in Hamburg as early as 1959.

such as 'Goodnight', a lullaby written for his son Julian, 'Revolution 1', 'Sexy Sadie' about the Maharishi, 'Dear Prudence' about Mia Farrow's sister who was with them in India, 'Happiness Is a Warm Gun' and 'Julia' – the only Beatles song where John performs alone with an acoustic guitar.

None of the Beatles went to college; in fact Paul was the only one who might have qualified. Their great area of knowledge and learning was popular music. They would travel across Liverpool, changing buses three times, to hear an American single they had heard someone had or to get someone to show them a new chord. They talked music, analysed its structure, discussed vocal techniques, identified individual players on anonymous session musician line-ups; they listened to it, they played it and they wrote it. The rest of the world did not command much attention. They were very young when they first began playing Hamburg – George was only seventeen – and being in a band, being 'the Beatles', was really the only thing they knew. Once they were managed by Brian Epstein all the normal everyday concerns were taken care of: they didn't have to cook or to shop for clothes or do anything except get from home to rehearsals, recording sessions, television shows, interviews or performances. Throughout the mad years of Beatlemania they were sheltered from normal life by a Liverpool support bubble consisting of Epstein, their roadies Mal Evans and Neil Aspinall, plus Peter Brown, Alistair Taylor and Tony Bramwell. Between them they took care of all the boys' needs: they controlled the groupies, filtered the drug dealers, chose couturiers, restrained courtiers and got the Beatles home in one piece. When Brian Epstein unexpectedly died they were cast adrift, their safety bubble burst.

John Lennon had already been showing signs of distress at being a Beatle; his dysfunctional upbringing had given him many demons, and the unnatural pressures of fame were beginning to crack the carapace. He had always been the closest of the Beatles to Brian, whom he regarded in part as his missing father figure, even though Brian was only six years older than him.

The other Beatles held up better initially, but Paul's break-up with Jane Asher in the summer of 1968 precipitated a crisis for him. Ever since moving to London in April 1963 Paul had lived with Jane for many years at her parents' home in Wimpole Street, where he had the security of an ordered, upper-middle-class intellectual lifestyle. He had Margaret Asher, Jane's mother, as his missing mother figure and the emotional security of his relationship with Jane. When Jane found him in her bed with Francie Schwartz, an American groupie, she ended the affair, and Paul appeared to have some sort of breakdown, often showing up at Alistair Taylor's flat in the middle of the night to cry on his shoulder. But Jane would not have him back, and he was soon with Linda Eastman. However, he never had quite the same self-confidence of the early years again. This affected his approach to Apple, and he managed to alienate many of the devoted staff. Paul arrived one morning in a long overcoat, unshaven and 'dark in mien and mood'. Paul called a staff meeting in Ron Kass's room. The staff crowded in and sat or leaned, wondering what he was going to say. Derek Taylor recalled Paul's opening words:

'Don't forget, you're not very good, any of you. You know that, don't you?' I had forgotten, I had. It had gotten to the point where I was really believing in myself, you know, really having a good time being me . . . I don't think I ever hated anyone as much as I hated Paul in the summer of 1968. Postcards would arrive at my house from America or Scotland or wherever, some outright nasty ones, some with no meaning that I could see, one with a postage stamp, torn in half and pasted neatly showing the gap between the two halves. Joan [Taylor's wife] received one bearing the words: 'Tell your boy to obey the school-masters,' and signed: 'Patron.' Far out.[6]

Paul had no experience in management and must have felt out of his depth: seeing tens of thousands of pounds being spent without proper controls or administration. Although Derek was by no means the worst culprit, Paul was right; there was a cavalier attitude in the press office: the easiest way to fob off someone who arrived and announced themselves as 'Hitler to see John Lennon' was to give them a drink. And Derek was probably too expansive in his largesse, but at least he was not selling the lead off the roof, as it turned out that the post boy was: he was always leaving the building with a bulging mail sack so no one suspected until it was too late. Apple desperately needed a man in charge (it was all men in those days). They had a managing director, Neil Aspinall, but were not prepared to let him get on with it. Taylor reported, 'These were the days when Neil Aspinall as Managing Director would come to my room in Apple in the middle of the day and collapse on the sofa and sit staring and staring. He tells me now it was fear.'[7]

It was not that the Beatles had been infantilized; just that they had never had a chance to grow up in the normal sense of knowing how much things cost, how to buy a bus ticket, all the everyday things that most people know almost instinctively. They were always 'the boys', even after Apple set up they were still 'the boys'. All of which was why the Beatles were probably the last people in Britain who should have attempted to run a company: they didn't have the slightest idea of how to go about it, and terrible mistakes were made. They had no knowledge of business or money, no understanding of management or delegation, no concept of budgets or costings or any of the other elements that are required to manage a company. They tried to hire people to do those things, but as long as they were all four joint managing directors they constantly countermanded each other's decisions, bickered and squabbled and made some appalling business choices. According to Derek Taylor, only slightly tongue-in-cheek, their only model for running a company was that of a northern mill owner.

Tensions quickly developed at Apple because there was no one in charge. On a practical level this meant that people like Peter Asher could not do their jobs properly. Peter told *Rolling Stone*, 'I was theoretically head of A&R, but I was answering to a board of governors who were never in the same place at the same time. Sometimes I would sign someone and nothing would happen. At the same time, one of the Beatles would sign someone and I didn't know about it. And they'd always be arguing with each other, and I was on the periphery of all the arguments.'[8] He soon found that, although he was head of A&R, he could not go out and sign someone; he needed a quorum of Beatles on his side, at least one but preferably two. The same went for getting approval for the artwork for album and single sleeves; the Beatles would all countermand each other and were never there at the same time to make a joint decision. Sometimes it resulted in direct action. On one occasion George Harrison, outraged to find that a partition he had ordered to be demolished had been reinstalled, found a hammer and smashed down an eight-foot by three-foot panel, showering Sylvia, a secretary, with plaster, wood and nails. By Christmas 1968 the Apple office was struggling to function.

Now it was winter, and Apple was preoccupied by the Christmas and New Year festivities. However, I did manage at some point to corner each individual Beatle and make sure that they all knew – and more importantly approved – of my plan to fly to the USA in January to record as many of the poets on my list as I could for Zapple. George simply said that it was Paul's and John's thing and nothing to do with him; I got the sense that he disapproved. Ringo said, 'Just get on with it', as if I was interrupting him. John and Yoko said they were 'behind the project 100 per cent' but were too busy with their own problems to contribute much to the discussion. Yoko and I did talk a bit about Charlotte Moorman, the 'topless' cellist, and Carolee Schneemann and a few other performance artists associated with Fluxus in New York, who we might be able to somehow present on record. Yoko wondered what 'Fluxus' George Maciunas would think of that, as he had blacklisted most of the New York female performance artists from his organization. I saw it as a challenge for the future, but we never had a chance to follow it up. When I reached New York I did receive a telegram from John and Yoko suggesting that I record Gregory Corso and Diane di Prima, both of whom were already on the list. These were undoubtedly Yoko's suggestions. I also worked closely with Ron Kass, head of Apple Records, Derek Taylor and, of course, Peter Asher, who had to approve studio rentals, travel expenses, budget and so on. Finally I telephoned Allen Klein in New York, and he yelled, 'I expected you here last week. Everything's arranged! Where were you?' He hadn't expected me and nothing was arranged, but the project did seem to be on. To do all this meant hanging around Apple for an inordinate amount of time, tracking people down and having meetings, and so I got to know the intimate details of the way the place was run, as well as gaining a working knowledge of what was in the press office drinks cupboard.

None of the Beatles went to college
. . . Their great area of knowledge
and learning was popular music.
They would travel across Liverpool,
changing buses three times, to hear
an American single they had heard
someone had or to get someone to
show them a new chord.

Chapter 5

Hells Angels

IT/47, January 1-16, 1969.

THE family heads of some of San Francisco's tribes have hit town on a mind-blowing London run. There are 13 of them in all, including a baby. There is Pete and Sweet William from Hell's Angels, Jonathan, Danny and Rock of The Grateful Dead, Spider, Slade and another Peter of the Pleasure Crews and Ken Kesey of the Merry Pranksters. . . and then there are their women - Blanc' ', Frankie and Sue. And last but not leas , there's Peter Zimmels, their spiritual adviser who was once a Buddhist monk.

There is something vital and vibrating about these meat athletes from America's last frontier. They have created a sense of family and a feeling of brotherhood among each other that is seldom seen here. Their shot is a down-to-earth, no-holds-barred honesty which could easily offend the unsuspecting but is a real turn-on for others. I got the impression that they found the English rather too 'cool'.

They swagger about like cowboys in their genuine Levi's, saddle boots and assorted head gear rambling on about their 'choppers' - the 74 cu. in., 1200 cc Harley Davidson bikes which Pete and Sweet William brought over with them - their love of the wide open spaces back home, and the rip-roaring crazy excitement which seems to emanate from San Francisco.

The purpose of their pleasure trip is to look around and see what is happening over here. In the summer they hope to bring over some fifty Hell's Angels, The Grateful Dead and other aspects of their scene in the hope of capturing, for us, the spirit of their way-out culture. England. . . Be prepared.

Lee Harris

Tumbleweed, Sweet William and their choppers

Photo: Gabi Nauseman.

Top: The Hells Angels arrive in town, as reported in *International Times*.

Bottom: Programme for Fillmore East, Bill Graham the concert promoter there, bankrolled the Angels' trip to the Beatles on pain of death (literally). Fillmore East was a rock venue on Second Avenue, near East 6th Street, which played host to some of the biggest names in rock, including a performance of John Lennon with Frank Zappa and the Mothers of Invention on 6 June 1971.

Hells Angels

IN SAN FRANCISCO ON 7 August 1967, on a Haight-Ashbury walkabout with Pattie, Neil Aspinall, Derek Taylor and 'Magic' Alex, George Harrison ran into Hells Angels Tumbleweed and Frisco Pete on the corner of Divisadero. In a friendly gesture George foolishly invited the Angels to visit, even giving them his card. They naturally took up the offer. It took them a while to get it together; money had to be raised for the trip, but this was forthcoming from Bill Graham, the impresario and concert promoter. Over the years he had received four bullets from the Angels, each representing a death threat caused by some slight or disrespect in their eyes. Graham had them displayed in a row: .357s, .44s on his desk. Now the Angels presented themselves in his office. It was payback time. Peter the Monk arrived and explained that they would take back the bullets in exchange for $1,000. Graham no doubt remembered how the New York Angels had hung him out of his second-storey office at the Fillmore East when he tried to stop them wearing their colours in the auditorium. Peter the Monk left with his money. On 4 December 1968 George sent round a memo that read:

> Hells Angels will be in London within the next week, on the way to straighten out Czechoslovakia. There will be twelve in number, complete with black leather jackets and motorcycles. They will undoubtedly arrive at Apple and I have heard they may try to make full use of Apple's facilities. They may look as though they are going to do you in but are very straight and do good things, so don't fear them or uptight them. Try to assist without neglecting your Apple business and without letting them take control of Savile Row.

It was initially intended to start the Zapple series with an album by Ken Kesey, whose Merry Pranksters had been one of the inspirations for the *Magical Mystery Tour*. Communications with him had been inconclusive, and he was not on my list of people to record in the first batch. However, Kesey had decided to attend the Grateful Dead-organized Hells Angels trip to London, which worked out perfectly. As I was just about to depart on my recording trip to the USA it was decided that Derek Taylor would produce Kesey's album in London; perhaps recording his impressions of the city or a live reading. It was up to him to decide. It was through Kesey, who sent a note to George Harrison, that Apple knew that the Angels were expected.

The first news of the arrival in Britain of thirteen family heads from some of San Francisco's tribes came in the form of a telephone call from Heathrow customs asking for £250 in shipping charges for two Harley Davidson choppers. Apple paid. The party consisted of Kesey, Peter Coyote from the San Francisco Mime Troupe, Peter the Monk (their spiritual adviser – a Buddhist monk turned Hells Angel, real name Peter Zimmels), Slade and Spider from the Pleasure Crew, Frisco Pete and Bill 'Sweet William' Fritsch and their 'old ladies' Blanhe and Frankie Hart a.k.a. Frisco Fran, two Deadheads Connie Bonner and Sue Swanson, and the Grateful Dead's two managers, Danny Rifkin and Rock Scully. The party had begun as soon as the Air India DC-8 took off on 23 December. There were not many passengers aside from the Angels on the overnight flight, so they took over the middle of the plane, let all the seatbacks down and covered them with their sleeping bags, the airline blankets and their coats and sat cross-legged in a giant circle. Kesey told them Northwest Indian and Eskimo stories, and someone produced a harmonica; they had a sing-song and a bit of jam session. David Dalton wrote, 'To complete the picture, Peter Coyote's injecting himself in the stomach with Vitamin B12 and methamphetamine. He's got hepatitis, and Doctor Feelgood, the famous New York City doctor, has given Peter his own secret remedy, a walking cure for hepatitis.'[1]

As the plane approached London in the early morning fog Kesey wrote in *Demon Box*, 'everybody realized that after our transatlantic antics a customs check was almost certainly coming up, and what couldn't be flushed had better be swallowed. Up to the bustling British customs table we floated, a big-eyed baker's dozen from America, in leather and furs and cowboy hats and similar fashionable finery. The weary officer sighed sorely at the sight, then politely searched us for three hours, even the cylinders of the two Harley Davidsons.'[2] Everyone had gone to the Nothing to Declare line except for Peter who went to the red zone with his brown paper bag filled with syringes and weird-looking bottles of medicine. The customs officers' eyes lit up with delight when they saw him. It took him a long time to pass through but not as long as it took to get the choppers out of customs.

Naturally the motley crew headed from the airport straight to 3 Savile Row in an assortment of Land-Rovers, cabs and motorcycles, some of which had been sent by Apple. Jimmy Clarke, the Apple doorman-cum-security guard, got an awful shock as they pulled up and the two Angels precariously balanced their choppers on their stands directly across the street from Apple's front door. He listened courteously to their request to see George and explained that he didn't doubt for one minute that they were indeed friends and guests of George's but that it was still early in the day and he was not in yet, so would they mind waiting. The tea ladies bustled around, making them tea and crumpets, and by the time Derek Taylor arrived they were all crashed out, having been up all night and jet-lagged, sleeping on couches in the waiting-rooms and in George's office.

George showed up at midday and gave them the tour of the building before disappearing. Ringo made a fleeting appearance. The Californians had made no plans, expecting to stay with George in his mansion. Derek Taylor had to explain that George's house was completely booked up but had he known they were coming things might have been different. Now the Apple staff had to sort out accommodation for thirteen. As the two Angels were the only ones actually invited by George to stay, they, their girlfriends and their bikes were sent to Ladbroke Grove in Notting Hill to stay with Apple press officer Richard DiLello – the 'House Hippie' – who shared a flat with Stanley Mouse the cartoonist and David Dalton, who had been commissioned to write the text for the Apple book to accompany the album *Get Back*. Most of the others were sent to a large ground-floor flat belonging to a friend of a friend of someone on Prince of Wales Drive in Battersea. Somehow space was found for everyone across town, although some of them stayed in a large room at the top of the Savile Row building that was already occupied by American hangers-on, who had managed to infiltrate the Apple office.

Paul's and John's declaration on prime-time television that they would help everyone had naturally attracted all manner of cranks and mentally disturbed people, all of whom had to be dealt with by Apple's long-suffering staff. This included a group of hippies called the Firedog Family from Fort Smith, Arkansas, led by 'Emily', who had arrived at the doorstep and somehow insinuated themselves into the building, where they had been given a large room in which they lived, ate and slept. Kesey was astonished that they had even made it through the front door as 'they were even scruffier than we were'. He described them in *Demon Box*. 'Half a dozen big bearded dudes with ragged grins, a bunch of naked noisy kids, and one woman – a skinny redhead on the sinewy side of thirty sporting a faded blue dress of hillbilly homespun with matching hicky twang. "We're the Firedog Family . . . I had this dream me and John was running side by side through the electric-blue waters of the Caribbean and he looked at me and says, 'Come Together.' . . . We know they is in the building . . . Y'know, don't you, that the Beatles is the most blessed people on earth? They are."'[3] The Angels were not particularly appreciated by those working at Apple, who were, after all, trying to run a record company. Apple director Peter Brown described them as 'a travelling entourage of smelly, stoned, long-haired Californian hippies in bells and love beads',[4] and most of the staff were outright scared of them.

Grateful Dead manager Danny Rifkin spent quite a bit of time at my place, but I don't recall if he was actually staying there. It was great to hear all about the San Francisco scene, and he wrote a report on it for *International Times*. We went to the Portobello Road market, and he wheeled a Victorian coal scuttle all the way back to Westminster. His most memorable line came when he finished rolling a joint on a tea tray, smoked it, then swallowed the tiny roach. 'Now your tray's clean, man!' he pronounced. I was delighted.

After sorting out their accommodation, and meeting George and Ringo (Paul was in New York, John was getting ready for the Apple Christmas party that evening), the Angels and their party set out to explore London and try out some of those British pubs. Meanwhile Sally and Diana, the Cordon Bleu cooks, spent the day cooking a 43-pound turkey and finishing the arrangements for their long-planned gourmet banquet to be held in the boardroom.

Christmas was a big event for the Beatles: they always made a special Christmas-themed record to send to members of their fan club; when they were touring they always did a Christmas Show at the Hammersmith Odeon; and Brian Epstein always laid on a fabulous Christmas party for their staff, complete with presents that Brian himself chose. The Beatles continued the tradition at Apple, and the internal memo issued for the Christmas party held on 23 December 1968 read:

In the middle of the party we will be visited by Ernesto Castro and April, entertainers to the Queen and the Duke of Cornwall and the late Sir Winston Churchill, MacDonald Hobley and others. Mr Castro is a conjurer, ventriloquist and children's entertainer. April is his assistant and also his wife and she plays guitar. So the idea is that all of us at Apple will bring our children and those of us who have no children are invited to bring a couple unless they can arrange to have one of their own in the meantime.

Over a hundred children attended the children's party, held at 2.30 p.m. in Peter Brown's office where they sang and danced, and consumed a mountain of sausage rolls, ice-cream and Christmas cake. Ernesto and April ended the show with a powerful rendition of the 'Lettuce Leaf Hop', and then the children went to meet John and Yoko, dressed identically as Mother and Father Christmas, in the press office where they handed out presents to staff and families of staff, 'ho-ho-ho-ing' and full of good cheer, assisted by Mary Hopkin, and a fun time was had by all.

Meanwhile those without children, the press and those who had already received their presents gathered in the press office in more or less two groups, those who were smashed on whisky and beer and, in the small back room, those who were smashed on pot and hashish. John and Yoko, out of their costumes, sat on the floor cross-legged, surrounded by Emily's Firedog Family, waiting for the food to be ready. Suddenly Frisco Pete, stoned out of his mind on hash and drink, pushed his way through the crowd with giant strides and stopped, glaring down at John Lennon. 'What the fuck is going on in this place?' he screamed. The room went silent, the enjoyable atmosphere immediately soured by this unwelcome intrusion. 'We wanna eat! What's all this shit about havin' to wait until seven?' The Angels had been drinking all day, and it had not occurred to them to eat so they were tired, jet-lagged and hungry. Alan Smith, a music journalist and the husband of Mavis Smith who had started work in the press office at Apple only two weeks before, stepped forward saying, 'Let's have a little consideration.' It was a mild rebuke, but in response Frisco Pete closed his fist and punched Alan in the face.

Kesey, who thought that Alan Smith worked for Apple, gave a colourful, and probably exaggerated, description of what happened next. 'The executive went somersaulting backward all the way to the wall, where he slowly slid down in a pile against the baseboard and lay there, like a rumpled rainbow. The room suddenly polarized, all the Englishmen springing to one side of the carpet to surround their clobbered countryman in an instant display of British pith, all the Yanks to the other.' Kesey took off his watch ready for a fight as Pete challenged the room. 'Anybody else?' he asked. Derek Taylor sent Richard DiLello to fetch Peter Brown who was, fortunately, just outside in the hall. Richard continued the story in his autobiography:

> Peter Brown glimpsed in two blinks what was happening. The House Hippie gulped and closed his eyes as Peter walked calmly up to the San Francisco chapter of the Hells Angels Motorcycle Club. Tapping him lightly on the shoulder, Peter Brown moved between John Lennon and Frisco Pete just as a fresh flow of verbal punches was about to begin. An audible intake of breaths circled the room.
>
> 'Now listen, Pete, we have every intention of feeding you and I apologize for the delay, but I was hoping you could appreciate that the kitchen staff have been working since 9:00 and they've been under considerable pressure. We're waiting for the caterers to finish laying the tables and it shouldn't take more than another ten minutes and then we can all go downstairs and gorge ourselves to death but please, I beg you, be patient.'[5]

Frisco Pete turned and abruptly left the room, so the Americans didn't have to beat anybody up. Unfortunately when the door to the boardroom was opened ten minutes later Frisco Pete charged in, grabbed the turkey, tore off a leg and began chomping on it. He and his fellow Americans demolished the feast, eating with their hands

Ken Kesey in full cowboy mode, dressed for the tourists in London (all his clothes were probably bought at Carnaby Street). Kesey, through his notorious acid tests, was the leading exponent of the sixties drug culture.

and drinking the fine wines from the bottle, leaving the cutlery and glasses unused. By the time the rest of the guests had filed in there was nothing left. Sally and Diana, who had spent weeks planning their gourmet Christmas dinner with all the trimmings, complete with candles and crackers, were devastated to see it all demolished. Tony Bramwell wrote, 'It looked like a battlefield. The Merry Pranksters had ruined the whole event and now they were seriously drunk and mean. They threw up on carpets and insulted their hosts. Enough was enough, and a few days later they were turfed out of the building by George who was very embarrassed.'[6]

There was a bit of a struggle when it came time for the Angels to leave and a few of the bigger men had to assist them out of the building. It was generally thought that next time George wanted to invite a bunch of thugs to Britain he should have them stay at his place, not the office. It was several days after Christmas when Frisco Pete and Sweet William left London, intending to go to Czechoslovakia to fight against the Russian-led Warsaw Pact invasion which ended the 'Prague Spring'. Styling themselves as 'freedom fighting gorillas' – their spelling – they headed off towards Harwich, intending to take a ferry to the Hook of Holland, but the English weather was too much for them, the snow and ice incapacitated their choppers, and they never even made it to the port. Presumably Apple paid to ship their choppers back to the balmy sun of California. The Russians were no doubt relieved.

Ken Kesey had originally arrived at Apple in nothing but the clothes he wore, an unwashed tunic and large cowboy hat, jeans and boots – no luggage. Tony Bramwell, as head of promotions, was given the job of making him look presentable to the media for interviews, photographs and so on, the usual press office stuff. As Bramwell wrote, 'With money no object, he soon got the knack of shopping. I can't say I blame him. It was all free, and Carnaby Street had some wonderful things to offer.'[7]

Kesey recorded nothing when the Angels were in town, he was too busy hanging out and exploring, but he returned to London in the new year with his wife Faye and their three children and borrowed a flat in Hampstead. He chugged around town in a borrowed 1958 Cadillac with huge fins, and each day he took the tube to Apple, where he had a desk and an IBM Golf-Ball typewriter (something much sought after in the building – being a published writer obviously gave him higher status than most). He was also given a portable tape-recorder, presumably a Uher 4000 Report, the best low-cost professional portable around at the time, as I doubt that even Apple would have trusted him with a Nagra. While I was away he borrowed my Revox A77 to play back his tapes, which made sense.

His album was to be called *Paperback Records* and was to consist of field recordings of his explorations of London with possibly some longer extracts from his books or new writing on the second side, but when Apple disintegrated so did his project. An interview in the *Evening Standard* in May 1969 reported, 'He's also here to make a record in a spoken-word series for Apple. But since their economy measures he's found himself without an office or cooperation. He's a little bitter about it, but he's carrying on with making the tapes anyway. "I write a lot. I just haven't written anything that pleases me for a long time. Nothing I've done communicates as well as tape does for me." He's a great Peter Pan of a fellow, quick-witted and very funny, and driving around London in his cowboy hat and wind-cheater he looks like some leftover from *Bonanza*.'

During Allen Klein's mass firings later, all of Kesey's tapes vanished, along with everything else that wasn't nailed down. Maybe he had copies. I hope so. With the closure of Zapple, Kesey left the IBM at the front desk but took his portable and my Revox A77 with him. I can't say that I blame him; he wanted to keep making tapes, and I doubt he had received an advance. In any case someone else would have probably stolen them if he had left them behind.

Ken Kesey had originally arrived
at Apple in nothing but the clothes
he wore, an unwashed tunic and
large cowboy hat, jeans and boots
- no luggage . . . As Bramwell wrote,
'With money no object, he soon got
the knack of shopping. I can't say
I blame him. It was all free and
Carnaby Street had some wonderful
things to offer.'

Chapter 6

East Coast

16 Lord North Street,

London S.W.1.

Ken & Betsy,
719 E. 9th,
New York 10009.   20th January 1969.

Dear Ken and Betsy,

Thanks for your letter. Short note to say I'll be
arriving in New York on the 29th of January on the Air India
flight 105 from London airport leaving London at 13.00 hours.
Should get in around 3.p.m. I think (?) so we can have afternoon tea together.

Look forward to seeing you,

                    Love,

                    Miles.

East Coast

IT WAS WITH SOME trepidation that I set off to record six albums for Zapple, given that my only experience had been to produce three spoken-word albums back in 1965, all recorded on a battered old hired Ferrograph operated by Ian Sommerville. I had some experience of tape editing from that time, and I had done a little more at the studio on Montagu Square. I had watched both Paul and Peter edit tapes at Wimpole Street, and they had shown me how to splice using a single-sided razor blade and a metal editing block. I had observed carefully during the times we had been allowed into the control room at Abbey Road to listen to playbacks and to watch George Martin at work on the mixing desk. I often talked to Peter Asher about record production and learned a lot from him about microphone techniques, how to avoid dry sounds, how to use equalization and so on, and I felt confident that I knew enough to make a few spoken-word records and even to add a few musical accompaniments or live recordings to make them more accessible to the general public. The studio technicians would do the miking up and would run the recorders; I just needed to know enough to be able to tell them what I wanted. Still, a certain amount of bluff was required.

Apple arranged my trip: an Air India 707, business class. I had been to New York two years before, in 1967, but the combination of modern technology and old-fashioned luxury travel still intrigued me: the stewards in white coats and the typed index card, reverently passed from row to row telling us what height and speed we were travelling at. I arrived at JFK amid flurries of snow. It was 29 January. I had arranged to stay with my friends Ken Weaver and Betsy Klein in Ken's apartment at 719 East 9th Street between Avenues B and C, where I had stayed previously. They picked me up in a battered old Ford. Later I learned that Apple had sent a limo to meet me; no one told me, and I had not realized that it was normal in the record business for executives to be treated this way. The limo would have caused quite a stir on East 9th Street, because in those days that part of Alphabet City was notoriously dangerous, with burnt-out cars littering the sidewalks, overflowing garbage cans and frequent knife fights in the streets; I had witnessed one from Ken's window the previous time I stayed there.

Ken was one of the people I hoped to record. His fellow Fug, Tuli Kupferberg, had released a spoken-word album, *No Deposit, No Return*, an album of 'found' poetry, on ESP-Disk in 1966, so I thought there must be a market for Ken's Tex-speak aphorisms. He was a Texan born on Galveston Island and had grown up in El Campo, a railroad camp set up to ship cows from the four big local cattle ranches. When I visited him he used to subscribe to the bi-weekly local *El Campo Leader-News* and would sit in his chair, surrounded by crushed beer cans, chuckling over the accidents, suicides and car wrecks of his home town. It really was the kind of newspaper that had headlines like 'Brewster's old sow got caught in the fence again last week'. Ken looked like a Hells Angel and indeed had a set of colours and later a Harley Davidson to go with them, but his appearance in 1969 was almost that of a rock star. The Fugs had spent several months, September and October 1968, touring Europe and were becoming quite well known. Bob Dylan claimed in an interview that they were his favourite group. Ken's hair fell in waves over his shoulders, he had a massive black beard that he liked to stroke thoughtfully and for street wear he wore a large leather cowboy hat and hand-tooled cowboy boots. He looked unbelievably fierce when he frowned, which was usually enough to scare people and stop trouble; he was capable of enjoying a good bar fight, but mostly this was a carapace covering a gentle soul. He was a brilliant raconteur, and I wanted to record an album with him of bar

Top left and right: East 9th Street in Alphabet City, then dangerous territory.

Bottom: Ken Weaver, drummer with the Fugs, preparing to be recorded. The Fugs were named after a euphemism for 'fuck' in Norman Mailer's *The Naked and the Dead*. The band originally comprised Ed Sanders, Tuli Kupferberg and Ken, although throughout the years they were joined by others.

conversation and humour in a Texan accent that was to be called Tex-speak.

I spent a couple of days recovering from jet lag, talking about the proposed album with Ken and trying to contact Charles Olson in Gloucester, Massachusetts, whom I also hoped to record before continuing my trip on to the West Coast. On Monday I made an appointment and went to see Allen Klein at ABKCO Industries, 1700 Broadway on West 54th Street – an anonymous, cheap-looking glass tower five blocks from Central Park. ABKCO was near the top, but the signage in the lobby was just bits of paper taped to a board, and at first I got off on the wrong floor to find myself in an undeveloped expanse of concrete and cables; the building wasn't even finished. The elevator rattled and shook and some of the secretaries at ABKCO were really scared of using it, never leaving the building except to go home. Despite his aggressive assurance that he was 'waiting for me', I never did get to see Klein on this trip. His doorkeeper was Iris Keitel, a stony-faced, aggressive woman who was both his personal assistant and mistress. Although the company was called ABKCO (the Allen and Betty Klein Corporation), Klein in fact lived with Keitel. For the first time in my life I actually had to shout at someone in an office; it was the only way to get through to Keitel that I had come all this way to make albums and had been assured by all four Beatles, as well as Klein, that there would be money and facilities waiting for me.

Only when I threatened to telegram the Beatles to complain about the reception I had received did she very begrudgingly hand over the money I needed, which had been there all along. Klein had only recently managed to insinuate himself into Apple, and although he was already acting as the Beatles' representative he was not, in fact, officially appointed as their 'adviser' until 8 February, so it was not really surprising that no one knew who was doing what and what role they should play. I have never been in an office where the

Ken's girlfriend, Betsy Klein. Betsy performed as a backing vocalist
on the Fugs' recordings and was an early supporter of the band.

atmosphere was so depressing and negative. Klein's relatives were all over the place, pawing at the secretaries, and Keitel sat like Cerberus outside Klein's locked door. A few days later, now that I had authorization, I was able to collect the portable Nagra I had requested before I left London from Capitol Records' studio. Ken and I recorded hours of his conversation at East 9th Street. It proved impossible to stop street noise leaking on to the tape, and looking back it would have been better to have accepted it and exploited it to lend atmosphere. Although the album was not released, much of the material appeared in written form in his 1984 book, *Texas Crude: The How-To on Talkin' Texan*, which was illustrated by his old friend Robert Crumb.

Ken's hair fell in waves over his
shoulders, he had a massive black
beard that he liked to stroke
thoughtfully . . . He looked
unbelievably fierce when he
frowned, which was usually enough
to scare people and stop trouble;
he was capable of enjoying a good
bar fight, but mostly this was a
carapace covering a gentle soul.

Chapter 7

The Big O

Charles Olson reading at Berkeley. Olson was to have a profound influence on
a generation of poets, including Ed Dorn, Robert Duncan and Robert Creeley.

The Big O

NOW I HAD THE Nagra tape-recorder – at a massive rental of $200 a week – but I still could not contact Charles Olson on the telephone. I sent cables and finally, at about 3 a.m., Olson called, waking everyone up. He said he could record the next day. I got up early, and Betsy Klein and I flew to Boston with the Nagra and a suitcase filled with tape. At the airport we encountered American bureaucracy: no one would rent us a car because I was paying but Betsy was driving, so in the end we took a cab to Gloucester, now best known as the setting for Sebastian Junger's *The Perfect Storm*. February is not the best time to visit Massachusetts. The streets of Gloucester were filled with snow, with only the main road being ploughed, and we had to walk the last few blocks to Fort Square, a spit of land projecting out into the harbour with about a dozen low white-painted wooden clapboard houses. The sea looked grey and very cold, and I had never before seen snow on the beach. Olson's apartment was on the top floor of a two-storey building at 28 Fort Square, reached by an outside wooden stair. His kitchen windows looked out over the rooftops to the harbour: a low mansard roof, electricity and telephone cables slicing the view. Olson was not in when we arrived, but he had left a note taped to the windowpane of the back door to say he would be back soon. It was written on the back of a threatening letter from a hospital about an unpaid bill. I was shocked; it always came as a surprise to remember that America did not have a national health system like we did at home. The white buildings were almost invisible under the deep snow. All sounds were muffled, the silence broken only by the occasional crunch of a passing delivery truck compressing the snow. Charles soon arrived carrying a large paper sack of groceries and let us in.

It was a railroad flat, with each room leading to the other. Every room was filled with books. Olson had been the rector of the famous Black Mountain College, and as a poet he is classed as a 'Black Mountain Poet' along with Robert Creeley and Ed Dorn, both of whom studied with him at Black Mountain. I first got to know him in London in 1967 when he was staying with Panna Grady in her enormous house overlooking Regent's Park. Olson worked best at night, or, rather, he did not notice the passage of time like most other people. His classes at Black Mountain often started at 11 p.m. and sometimes ran through until the next afternoon. He was a brilliant teacher. At Panna's house guests would arrive around eight in the evening and wait for him to get up. He would talk all through his breakfast – three or four eggs, a huge pile of bacon and toast – and they would leave around one or two in the morning. By then Charles's brain was going flat out and he would settle in for a long night's work. I wanted to record him because, unlike many of his contemporaries, he had no spoken-word records out and was approaching sixty – he was born in 1910. His poetry is more difficult to read than most, so I suggested some of the more accessible ones, but ultimately it was up to Charles what he read. In fact he stuck close to my suggestions: poems from his new collection, *Maximus IV, V, VI*[1] and a bit from one of my favourite books, *The Mayan Letters*,[2] which mixes archaeology, history and poetry in one slim volume; he read letters 13, 7 and 5. You can get an idea of Olson's work from his 1956 essay 'A Foot Is to Kick With' about trying to find the ending for a poem: 'You wave the first word. And the whole thing follows. But — You follow it. With a dog at your heels, a crocodile about to eat you at the end, and you with your pack on your back trying to catch a butterfly.'

Charles was a big man, tall (six feet eight inches), although now a little stooped and broad in chest, but not at all overweight. His hair and two-day growth of stubble was white. His friends called him

MAXIMUS POEMS
IV, V, VI

CHARLES OLSON

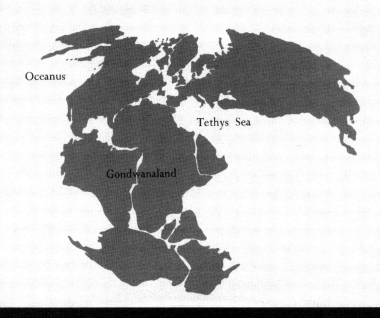

Oceanus

Tethys Sea

Gondwanaland

Olson's *Maximus* poems, which Miles was keen to feature on the record. He started to write the collection in the 1940s and continued to revise it until his death. This volume was published in 1968, with a posthumous edition being published in 1975. However, drafts found after his death indicate that the epic remained unfinished.

'the Big O'. He told me, 'The first time I realized that I was larger than the ordinary was once when I was running down a hill in Boston to catch a bus, and as I passed, a little black boy said, "My God, there goes Goliath!"' and he roared with laughter, a shout that came rumbling up from deep in his chest. His conversations were filled with these laughs. I described the apartment in the sleeve notes to the Folkways[3] release of the recording in 1975:

> Charles used to hold forth, propped against the huge refrigerator. Everything was in the most almighty muddle, papers, books, dishes, jars and boxes, even a storage jar of dried peyote mushrooms, all mixed up together. The window frames had pencil notes of lists of ships and cargoes, forgotten ships' captains and first mates and the customs duties they paid – long lists fading in the thin winter sun, obscured by a thin film of dust. The walls, too, had notes in Charles's thin, illegible handwriting, details of Dogtown and who built which house where.

There was a deep silence; the snow seemed to suspend time, and it was almost a shock to look through the snow-flecked windows over the white rooftops and see boats arriving at Gloucester Harbor under the white sky. The living-room bookcases were full to overflowing, jammed with coffee-ringed first editions. One book I pulled from a shelf had a letter from Ezra Pound used as a bookmark with several manuscript poems included. Magazines and journals were piled on the floor to table height and used as such. Charles's typewriter was balanced precariously in a little nest amid all the papers over by the window. I continued my description:

> The bedroom had a strange feeling of lack of use, stale air, sun warmed dust. The air outside in late January so cold we couldn't open a window. Strange in the warm rooms to feel the window-

panes ice-cold. In the total silence, broken only by the fridge thermostat and our own voices, so clear and loud without traffic noise or transistor rock to hide and dull them. There was so much to say. On our first night we did nothing but talk over a Chinese takeaway. The Nagra remained in its travelling case. Charles must rank along with Wilde and Strachey as a great conversationalist.

His talk ranged from geologic time to the importance of a sense of place. The trade between England and New England in the eighteenth century – he enjoyed the fact I came from Gloucestershire and here we were in Gloucester, Massachusetts – and gossip about Allen Ginsberg, Tim Leary and other mutual friends. He discussed Truman and Melville, the Fugs, Janis Joplin – whom he loved – and *Origin* magazine. The next day I searched for the best place to record. Although all the books tended to absorb some of the edge, our voices were clear.

Eventually I set up shop in his bedroom where the fridge couldn't get itself on tape. Charles sat in an upright chair, which creaked alarmingly but was the only possible one for him to use, so he said. In the dead of night we were sometimes disturbed by the muffled roar and crunch of snow as a truck slowly passed by. The room contained a long trestle table stacked two deep in maritime books, arranged spine up; hundreds of books, making the table sag, and to which I added a directional microphone. I arranged it as close as I dared to avoid Charles's gesticulations as he read and the fading as he looked away or down at the page. I sat on the floor by the door with my headphones and followed the text. Betsy sat in the living-room reading.

The first thing Charles found was that his speaking voice was not at all how he had imagined it to be. He had never listened carefully to a recording of it before and found it terribly lifeless, dry and boring.

Previous pages and above: Photographs taken by Miles during the recording of Charles Olson's *Maximus IV, V, VI* at Fort Square, overlooking the harbour in Gloucester, Massachusetts. Olson would work only at night.

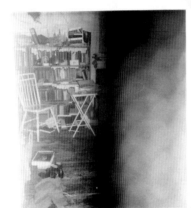

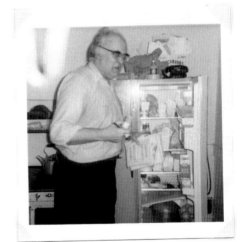

For a while I thought he was going to back out of the project altogether. The room's acoustics did make it drier than usual, but I explained that we could fix this to a certain extent in the mixing. Fortunately he decided to work with it and took care to read at the best possible speed with inflections and emphasis in the right places and careful pronunciation of unusual words, just as he took infinite care to arrange the words of his poems on the page in just the right places. Sometimes, even in the later recordings, he would catch his voice becoming dry and deep and would laugh out loud at himself. I have left one such false start at the beginning of the poem 'I Am the Gold Machine', a poem which gave us a lot of trouble and of which we did more than a dozen recordings.

We did a lot of takes that first day, and by the end of the session his voice was gone. Charles listened carefully to each one, head cocked to one side, attentive. To help his reading I marked up the books with musical notation marks for 'speed up' and 'slow down', used in this case to indicate volume, and underlined passages for greater emphasis and words that he normally slurred when reading. I conducted him by waving my arms about and pursing my lips to get him to give certain words more stress or raise his voice. After a night's work he got the hang of it and we knew how we were going to do it. He insisted, however, that we erase the tapes, which I did, and so the next day we started afresh. We mostly recorded poems from his new book *Maximus IV, V, VI*, which, luckily, I had brought with me as he had not yet received his copies from the publisher Cape Goliard in London because of a British postal strike. The three *Mayan Letters* were my request, although by the time he was through making asides and verbal annotations he had certainly made them his own again. In the following two nights we sailed through everything I was hoping to record, getting most things in one or two takes.

Charles was lonely and not in good health; he lived alone, and because many people regarded him as unapproachable weeks would sometimes go by without him seeing anyone other than his immediate neighbours. He seemed happy to see us and did not mind our intrusion on his privacy; he could do no work while we were there because of the layout of the rooms. He told me that his work output had halved since his wife died twelve years before. The whole time we were there he received only one telephone call, from his daughter Katherine. He told me he was worried that he would not be able to leave her anything and was shocked when I suggested that the Ezra Pound letters and first editions were worth a great deal. In my sleeve notes I wrote:

> Charles had been in the same house so long that he had stopped seeing it. We talked about the various shipping channels into the harbour, and he talked at length about a large map of Gloucester Harbor that he had annotated extensively. He sat on the bed with the map pinned to the wall behind him, and became a little irritated that we couldn't catch what he was saying. When he turned to look at the chart he realized it was blank. The sun had bleached it away forever, a sagging yellowing sheet, dust-marked and fly-spotted. How long was it since Charles had actually looked with interest and inquisitiveness around his own bedroom? He made a joke, but I could see deep down then he knew he was dying.

The recordings were a success. They sounded as I had wanted them to, as if Charles had simply read them off with no preparation, in spontaneous performance. It was the only recording 'for posterity', as he put it, that Charles ever made. Other tapes exist, fortunately, but they are often marred by drink, drugs or the technical problems of live recordings in those days: breaks in the tape, faulty microphone connections. The record was Charles reading his poems as he want-ed them read, and I felt enormously privileged to have produced it for him. We left after four days, and he gave me a copy of the *hors commerce* edition of *Human Universe* as a commemorative gift, with his annotations on some of the essays. I was very touched. Charles died a year later on 10 January 1970; he was only fifty-nine. A few months after his death I was staying on Allen Ginsberg's farm in upstate New York when Allen came into my bedroom early in the morning having just opened that day's post. He thrust a photograph in my face. It was a deathbed picture of Charles, looking peaceful in death. 'Ha! That'll get rid of your hard-on,' chortled Allen. Ginsberg knew and loved Olson. This was his way of sharing our mutual sadness at his death.

The living-room bookcases were
full to overflowing, jammed with
coffee-ringed first editions. One
book I pulled from a shelf had a
letter from Ezra Pound used as a
bookmark with several manuscript
poems included.

Chapter 8

The Poetry Farm

Allen Ginsberg in the kitchen of the Committee on Poetry farm in Cherry Valley, upstate New York. Allen bought the farm to serve as a haven for poets and friends. Many illustrious figures stayed there, including Lawrence Ferlinghetti, Gregory Corso, Gary Snyder, Robert Creeley, Bob Rosenthal and Barbara Rubin, among others.

The Poetry Farm

ALLEN GINSBERG HAD RECENTLY bought a farm in upstate New York and was spending his first winter there. It was at East Hill, six miles to the east of Cherry Valley, a small community of less than 1,000 people about eighty miles west of Albany, the state capital. The only way there, as I didn't drive, was to take the 6 a.m. bus from the Port Authority; a six-hour trip. Allen's boyfriend Peter Orlovsky was there to meet me when the bus pulled up in front of Crane's drugstore, where we sat on stools and had a malted milk in a store straight out of a *Saturday Evening Post* cover. In fact, the whole village was like that: white picket fences and white clapboard buildings with porches out front, some with swing chairs, all covered in deep snow. Peter drove me to the farm in his '56 Chevrolet, which of course fitted right in.

I needed to discuss Allen's proposed recording of William Blake's *Songs of Innocence and of Experience*, about half of which he had set to music. I was familiar with the Benjamin Britten and Ralph Vaughan Williams settings, but I knew there were many more out there. The tape he sent me showed that he was not going for a 'high art' interpretation but something closer to the music that Blake himself composed and sang in the pubs of Soho.

The Poetry Farm, as it was known, was in the middle of a hundred acres of meadowland surrounded by state forest, a two-storey, four-bedroom house with a separate wing off the kitchen where Peter and his new girlfriend, Denise, lived (Allen's social arrangements were complicated). Next to the living-room stood a traditional red-and-white barn where the horse and Bessie the milk cow lived. Peter and Gordon Ball, the film-maker, now farm manager, had tried to insulate the bedrooms by installing wooden tongue-and-groove panelling in each one, but with no heating system they were still bitterly cold. However, the Aladdin oil lamps gave out a lot of heat as well as light, and downstairs there was an Ashley wood-stove.

There was no electricity, but there was a telephone. By law the telephone company had been compelled to install a line, albeit a party line. The phone was just inside the kitchen door on the windowsill, and Allen for some reason sat in a tiny child's chair next to it, furiously dialling the *New York Times*, his publishers, his editors, his booking agents for readings, hours at a time and the other party-liners could never get through. Allen originally bought the place to get Peter away from his amphetamine dealers into a healthy outdoor atmosphere and also hoped that Jack Kerouac might move there to dry out, but Kerouac would never leave his mother and died of drink later that year.

Allen was on crutches, the result of a car crash in early December after delivering Lawrence Ferlinghetti to the airport. He had been hospitalized with a fractured hip and four broken ribs, but now, a month later, he managed to show me around. The snow prevented him from showing me his pride and joy, the gravity pump that provided water to the farmhouse. Down the hill from the house was a well, at the bottom of which was a spring and a gravity pump. The pump gathered water until the weight was enough to shoot a cupful up the hill to a tank buried above the house, seventy times an hour. The weight of the spring water alone was the driving force.

Allen could still get up the stairs to his room, which looked like something out of the nineteenth century: a desk lit by a pair of oil lamps, wooden coat rack behind the door, a big seven-drawer chest, a large wooden-framed bed with a woven Indian blanket and a portrait of Walt Whitman on the wall. Downstairs the living-room had a very comfortable feel with a big busted couch and colourful rugs bought at local barn sales. By the window hung a Tibetan thanka, brought back from India by Allen in 1963, the only one not stolen by Lower East Side junkies. There was an old-fashioned wooden pump organ, originally from a church, now used by Allen in the composition of his music. Lee Crabtree from the Fugs had taught Allen the basics of musical notation and a series of simple chords. This was what I had come for, and all through the afternoon and evening Allen sent halting windy notes whistling into the run-down old room to accompany his deep basso voice, the pedals making a terrible racket as he pumped furiously with his feet. It grew dark early, and the oil lamp on the organ was lit. A solitary moth circled its glass shaft. In the sleeve notes for the album Allen explained how he wrote the music:

> The songs were first composed on tape recorder, improvised on pump organ in farmhouse upstate NY in two nights after returning from Democratic Convention 1968 Tear Gas Chicago . . . The purpose in putting them to music was to articulate the significance of each holy and magic syllable of his poems; as if each syllable had intention. These are perfect verses, with no noise lost or extra accents for nothing. I tried to hear meanings of each line spoken intentionally and interestedly, and follow natural voice tones up or down according to different emphasis and emotions vocalized as in daily intimate speech.

He played all through the afternoon and continued after a break for dinner. The tootling, wheezing organ was perfect for Allen's hesitant playing and 'folk' approach to the music. Peter Orlovsky, recovering from amphetamine addiction, still had his 'leper's voice' as he called it (after the wails of the lepers he encountered when he and Allen lived in India), and his wildly out-of-tune enthusiastic duets were clearly going to pose a problem on some of the songs. But I figured we could deal with that in the studio. I loved what Allen had created; it would be a challenge to record, although one I looked forward to. We decided to record it in the summer, but first we needed a professional arranger, because many of the songs lent themselves to multi-instrumentation, and space for rehearsals in the city. However, there was plenty of time, and I left Cherry Valley satisfied that the Zapple project was now well under way.

This was what I had come for, and
all through the afternoon and
evening Allen sent halting windy
notes whistling into the run-down
old room to accompany his deep
basso voice, the pedals making
a terrible racket as he pumped
furiously with his feet. It grew
dark early, and the oil lamp on
the organ was lit. A solitary
moth circled its glass shaft.

Chapter 9

The First Trip: LA - Bukowski

Apple had offices in the famous Capitol Tower just north
of the Hollywood and Vine intersection.

The First Trip: LA - Bukowski

I FLEW INTO LAX on a Friday evening, too late to see anyone at the Capitol Tower, where Apple had an office. I had not forewarned anyone I was coming, so from the airport I telephoned the local underground newspapers. Art Kunkin, the editor of the *Los Angeles Free Press*, was out and no one seemed particularly friendly, even though they had published quite a bit of my work, so I phoned the newer *Open City*, where I had also published but knew no one. They were delighted to hear from someone from *International Times* and said to come straight on over. They were on Melrose in what looked like a converted body shop. There was a huge psychedelic mural covering the whole of the back wall, but there was something too crude, something unconvincing about it. John Bryan, the editor, laughed at my puzzled expression. The building had been used as the set for an underground newspaper in a cheap Hollywood exploitation movie about hippies, and now it was being used by a real underground paper – a brilliant Hollywood reversal. The *Open City* staff were wonderfully friendly, and I was immediately offered a place to stay and every kind of hospitality. I finished up with Mike Hodell, over in Silver Lake. It helped that I was in Los Angeles to record Charles Bukowski who had a regular column called 'Notes of a Dirty Old Man' in *Open City*. I had only been in California a few hours, but it seemed very foreign. I loved the climate and the palm trees and the laid-back attitude everyone had: a far cry from the speedy New Yorkers in their snow-covered streets I had left just a few hours before. I found the six hundred miles of freeways extraordinary; there seemed to be no centre to the city, and I soon found out that it was not regarded as unusual to drive fifty miles to see a concert. I spent the weekend with the *Open City* folks and on Monday presented myself at the

Capitol Tower at Hollywood and Vine. I loved the building; it looked like a stack of singles on an autochange: twelve floors, the bottom one ready to be whisked away and played.

Apple had a large office there, but no one from London had yet been over to see them, and they were desperate for news and information. Sadly I was not able to help them much as, aside from Peter Asher, Ron Kass, Derek Taylor and the Beatles themselves, I didn't know the other staff very well as I never had to deal with them. None the less, the American staff did everything they could to help me, hiring studio time in San Francisco, arranging car rental there, renting a portable tape-recorder for my Bukowski album. Just like the London office, ever since Paul and John had gone on American television saying they wanted to help people get a contract the American Apple office had been inundated with tapes. There were huge cupboards full that no one knew what to do with. I suggested they weed them out and send the more promising ones to Peter in London, as no one in Los Angeles could make decisions about them. I had a meeting with Jim Mahoney, Apple's West Coast publicist. He had sent out a press release on 3 February, a couple of weeks before I arrived, introducing the Zapple label. It read:

Beatles to introduce Zapple, new label and recording concept.

On May 1, just two weeks short of the first anniversary of the formation of Apple Corps Ltd and its Apple Records division, the Beatles company will introduce a new label and recording concept.

The label will be called Zapple and it will emphasize a series of 'spoken-word' albums and some music releases of a more wide-ranging and esoteric nature. Price of the Zapple albums will generally be $1.98 or $4.98, depending on the type of release.

Zapple will be a division of Apple Records, which is headed by Ron Kass, who is also chief executive for all Apple music activities. Supervising the Zapple program will be Barry Miles, a British writer-intellectual in his late twenties.

The first three releases on the Zapple label are now being pressed and include:

1. A new John Lennon-Yoko Ono album entitled *Unfinished Music No. 2 – Life with the Lions*

2. A George Harrison composed-produced electronic music album which was recorded with a Moog

3. A spoken-word album recorded by poet-writer Richard Brautigan

Other well-known writer-poets already committed to Zapple releases include: Lawrence Ferlinghetti – America's best-selling 'serious' poet; poet-playwright Michael McClure; veteran literary figures Kenneth Patchen and Charles Olson; and poet-essayist Allen Ginsberg. Additionally, Zapple will release one of the late Lenny Bruce's last concerts as an album.

It is the hope of Apple Corps Ltd that the new label will help pioneer a new area for the recording industry equivalent to what the paperback revolution did to book publishing.

The company is now studying new market ideas for the label, which it hopes to eventually retail in outlets where paperback books and magazines are sold; university and college outlets will also be emphasized in Zapple's distribution plans.

Discussions are now in progress with several world figures, as well as leaders in the various arts and sciences to record their works and thoughts for the label. The Beatles plan to tape several discussion sessions amongst themselves as an album release – probably for the fall. It is assumed that Zapple will have little difficulty attracting those people who might not normally record albums because of the general educational tone of the project.

There were two secretaries at Apple in the Capitol Tower with literally nothing to do, so they were delighted to have some work. I asked them to show me around town. The music clubs welcomed us with open arms, moving people from their seats to give us the best tables, proffering free drinks and all of them asking about 'the boys'. I said the boys were doing all right. One of the secretaries, Pat Slattery, drove me to see Bukowski in her green Mustang.

Charles Bukowski ('Buk') lived at 5126¼ De Longpre Avenue in East Hollywood, between Normandie and Kingsley. Sunset Boulevard was one block to the north, and the hazy view from Normandie looking north was of Griffith Park and the Observatory. The buildings were mostly single storey, low, with some old-style courts. There were rows of dusty, untended palm trees, chain-link fences tangled with weeds, and strands of plastic and torn super-market bags, guarded waste lots filled with broken bottles, crushed cigarette packs and yellow palm tree fronds. Walls were topped with razor wire and twisted barbed wire. Crumbling concrete garages, peeling billboards and stucco houses lined a street made from huge cracked concrete slabs, chipped at the edges and with utility cables and tall scruffy palms, some of which had died and rotted. It was the seedy side of Hollywood, and it was just as I had expected and hoped it would be.

Another iconic image of Bukowski taken by Sam Cherry. Here Buk stands on the pavement in the Skid Row neighbourhood of downtown Los Angeles. Sam photographed Bukowski many times, and Bukowski once cited Cherry's tough character as an influential component in his creation of his own tough-guy persona and protagonists. Cherry's son, poet Neeli Cherkovski, and Bukowski became lifelong friends, eventually starting their own literary magazine.

Bukowski's house was a single-storey stucco building with an open porch in a row of four identical houses set back off the street with a similar row opposite. A rusting '57 Plymouth was parked next to the house on a patch of hardened earth that might once have been a lawn and which housed a large trash bin overflowing with beer cans. The front door was glass, divided into sixteen panes, with a further eight panes on either side, a design echoed by the front window. The screen door opened directly into his living-room, about twenty feet long and twelve feet wide; the shades were drawn. To the left was an old sofa with the stuffing sticking out, next to which was a rickety bookcase made from wooden shelves supported by stacks of red bricks and cinder blocks salvaged from the street; it was filled with books, magazines – mostly small literary magazines – racing forms and newspapers. A pile of car tyres took over one corner – obviously inside to stop them being stolen; these were filled with empty crushed beer cans. There was a fireplace on the right and a dusty old rug. On the short back wall across from the front door was Buk's big wooden desk. Over the desk was a rack of pigeon-holes, a big wooden structure with ten compartments in each row containing various types of stationery, presumably thrown out of the post office (where he worked) at some point and salvaged by Buk. Next to the door, on its own office desk sat Buk's legendary 'typer', a pre-war, battered, sit-up-and-beg, black cast-iron Remington; dusty but for the carriage and keys which were polished by use. It was surrounded by cigar butts and ash, crumpled paper and more crushed beer cans. Thousands of poems and letters had emerged from this powerful machine: his columns for *Open City*, as well as stories and poems sent out to every little mimeo magazine that asked for work, from San Francisco to Germany and Japan.

Bukowski was forty-nine but looked ten years older; an extremely severe case of acne vulgaris, which had often put him in hospital as a child, had left his face, neck and shoulders a battlefield of scars.

His hairline was receding, and he wore a short, neatly trimmed beard and moustache. He was friendly and welcomed us in.

He explained that most people called him Hank. 'Otherwise, it's Buk,' he said. 'That's "Buke" as in "puke", not "Buk" as in "fuck".' He slipped out of the door, and we watched him half run down the block. He returned shortly with a six-pack of Miller's in glass bottles. With a bottle in his hand he was able to relax. He had written so much that I let him decide pretty much what he wanted to record. There were a few short stories I had read in his *Open City* column that I liked, and I suggested them. One sticking point was that Buk refused point-blank to go into a recording studio: he was too shy, he said; he was sure he would mess things up and embarrass himself, even though I assured him it would just be me and my assistant and an engineer there. I later learned that he would also not pick people up from the airport in case he got things wrong and went to the wrong place. At this time he was still working the night shift at the Los Angeles Post Office – the subject of one of his best books, *Post Office* – and had not yet done a public poetry reading. He seemed completely exposed to life, at full strength, with no shielding or defence mechanisms. This gave him his valuable insight but left him vulnerable and open to being hurt.

The solution was to set him up with a recording facility at home. I returned with an Ampex 3000, a microphone, mic stand, headphones and twelve reels of tape. Once again he insisted that he must work alone. 'Just show me how the machine works, and I'll curl up on the rug with some packs of beer and my books and turn on the machine . . .' We left him to it. He had made home recordings previously. Before we left he gave us both copies of his latest book, *Notes of a Dirty Old Man*. He wrote nicer things in Pat's copy than in mine.

Nine days later I returned, this time with Valerie Estes, my assistant whom I hired when I reached San Francisco, in a blue rented Mustang. Buk was there with a bit of a hangover.

Miles

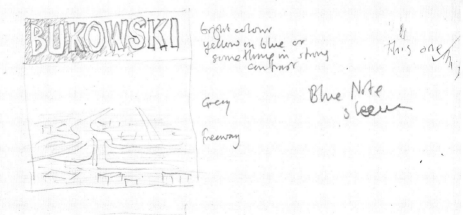

Bright colour
yellow on blue or
something in strong
contrast

this one ↙

Grey

Blue Note
sleeve

freeway

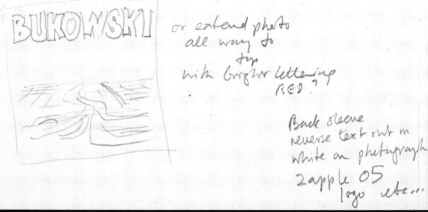

or extend photo
all way to
top
with brighter lettering
RED ?

Back sleeve
reverse text out in
white on photograph
2apple 05
logo etc...

A worn-out-looking woman with thick black hair, wearing black fishnet stockings with a few holes in them and a black slip, immediately retired to the bedroom in the back without introducing herself. She emerged shortly afterwards, fully dressed, and left. At the door Buk pressed some crumpled notes into her hand 'for car fare'. Nothing in the room had changed, and at first I was alarmed. But it was done; every reel was used – six hours of material – and he had even attempted to record 'on the other side' before he realized that professional machines are full track and he was just wiping out what he had previously recorded. He said to be sure to listen to the story called 'The Fire Station' which he thought had come out well. This time I had brought a six-pack of Miller's, so we talked a bit about his old car and his anxieties about giving up his job at the post office and going on to a retainer from his new publisher, John Martin at Black Sparrow Press. I thought it was a good idea, and shortly afterwards this is what he did, resulting in an explosion of work and his eventual fame. Back at the Capitol Tower we played the tapes. Buk was right. 'The Fire Station' was superb, and there was plenty of great material there for an album, including one interlude when Buk shouted abuse at his landlord from the window. The tapes were interspersed with the sound of bottles being opened, which was just the sort of thing I was looking for to get away from the formality of most poetry readings.

He explained that most people called him Hank. 'Otherwise, it's Buk,' he said. 'That's "Buke" as in "puke", not "Buk" as in "fuck".'

Chapter 10

The First Trip: SF – Brautigan

Richard Brautigan at Golden State Recorders during the making of *Listening to Richard Brautigan*. Brautigan had gone from being an unknown Haight-Ashbury poet to an acclaimed author on the publication of *Trout Fishing in America*.

The First Trip: SF - Brautigan

IN SAN FRANCISCO IT had seemed most economical to block book a series of sessions at Golden State Recorders at 665 Harrison Street, three blocks south of Market between 2nd and 3rd Streets in what was then a run-down, slightly dangerous area. Golden State came highly recommended, and we were lucky to book in as they were the only recording studio in town comparable to New York or Los Angeles studios even though it was a four-track. San Francisco had not yet developed its recording industry, and most groups like the Grateful Dead or Jefferson Airplane still went to Los Angeles to record, but four-track was fine for spoken word. Golden State had been there since 1964 and still had an original Ampex model 200, the first tape-recorder built in the USA. They already had a number of bookings, so I filled in the space around them, thinking that as I intended working on all three albums simultaneously there would always be work to do on one of them. We were fortunate in having a superb engineer, Mike Vance, who was sympathetic to what we were trying to do.

Before I left for the recording trip there had been quite a bit of correspondence between Richard Brautigan and myself regarding his album. He had told me he wanted to do an 'album that would be my vision of life in America. It would be a kind of audio novel using words, music and sounds.'[1] My secretary, Sarah Fenwick, replied, acknowledging receipt of his letter and saying, 'Miles is in Italy at the moment but should be back shortly and will be writing to you then – I am sure he will like your idea of the record as that is exactly the type of thing he wants to do.'[2] It was, and I wrote at once to confirm that I liked the idea. As his was the most worked out of the albums, I called him, then took a cab straight to his place at

2546 Geary from the airport. Richard Brautigan's apartment occupied the entire first floor of a shabby three-storey, stucco-fronted clapboard house with a wooden pediment containing a diamond attic window. A three-window bay overlooked the busy street, and a steep stoop led to the entrance porch with two doors, one of which led to Richard's entrance hall. His door had a small window set in it, on which were taped a Digger dollar and a feather; Richard had been closely involved with the Diggers, the Free Store and the Communications Company: all 1,500 copies of his book *All Watched Over by Machines of Loving Grace* (1967) were given away free.

It looked like a typical bachelor pad. The big high-ceilinged living-room looked well lived in with posters for readings, handbills for the Fillmore West, drawings and memorabilia tacked on the walls, a round oak table, stained with coffee-cup rings, was surrounded by an odd assortment of chairs, some of which looked positively unsafe to sit on. A fishing pole was propped in the corner, and a museum of odd objects lined the mantelpiece of the non-working fireplace and shelves: a klaxon, feathers, collages, a printing card announcing 'You have been assisted by a member of the Hells Angels'. I had one of those from Frisco Pete, given to me on his visit to Apple. The ceiling had been painted white, and the lining paper was peeling off in great sheets. The small kitchen still had its original bulky porcelain sink with a brass faucet, and the faded linoleum looked almost as old. The refrigerator contained little but beer. His bedroom was filled by a big brass bed.

Richard was tall and gangling, much taller than I expected, possibly six feet six inches, like Olson, only much thinner. He had startlingly white skin, long, fluffy shoulder-length blond hair that stuck out at the sides and a drooping moustache. His fingernails were bitten to the quick. His voice had a lilting, slightly strangulated quality making each sentence very precisely annunciated. He liked to affect an old-timer look, with a wide-brimmed hat and waistcoat as if he were a forty-niner. Although filled with objects, the apartment was tidy, with dust in the corners but none on the built-in bookcases, which were filled with mimeographed poetry magazines, slim volumes of verse and small press items. His IBM Selectric had a plastic dust cover over it, and on his big wooden desk he kept his pencils arranged in a neat row. Order and counting things were the subjects of many of his short stories.

His best pal, the novelist Keith Abbott, seemed to be always there. It was Keith who drove Richard around, as he did not drive. Richard's girlfriend, Valerie Estes, was also there when I arrived, and at Richard's suggestion I hired her as my assistant. I had asked if he knew anyone who could help me out, and it made sense for them to keep the money in the family. Similarly it seemed better to pay Valerie to stay at her apartment rather than pay for a hotel, so by the evening I had an assistant and a comfortable place to stay at 1429 Kearny, near Coit Tower in North Beach.

I had first been drawn to Brautigan's work by his book *A Confederate General from Big Sur*, with its Larry Rivers reproduction on the dust wrapper. I liked his quirky, whimsical humour and the weird twists of his poetry. Richard and I had very similar ideas about how the album should go: poetry but with a public surface to draw the listener in. We didn't want sound effects, but we thought it would be good to record the actual stream he wrote about in *Trout Fishing in America* and that miscellaneous sounds of everyday life in his apartment would make good fillers between the tracks. We wired up Richard's kitchen, filled the fridge with beer and taped hours of his conversation with Keith Abbott, as well as Richard answering the telephone, brushing his teeth, opening beer, eating and going about his daily business; all in keeping with the title *Listening to Richard Brautigan*.

The tracks were all done in the studio, and for 'Love Poem' I suggested that he read it twice over, as it was so short. He had a

STEREO ST-424

LISTENING TO RICHARD BRAUTIGAN

Richard Brautigan was born January 30, 1935 in Tacoma, Washington.
His memories at the age of four included: the-waking-up-in-the-morning,
what's-for-breakfast? poverty of the American Depression, the exotic war
between Japan and China, trace remembrances of the Spanish Civil War,
and the German Army of the Third Reich marching into Poland on
September 1, 1939. Since then he has enjoyed thirty more years of life
in the Twentieth Century. Right now he lives in San Francisco.
His telephone number is 567-3389.

Above and opposite: The album sleeve for *Listening to Richard Brautigan* as finally
released on Harvest Records. Note on the back sleeve Richard's added sticker
claiming co-production. The album is still available from Collector's Choice
Music on CD, the sleeve of which contains a detailed list of what Brautigan read
track by track. This photograph of the LP is courtesy of Todd Gunderson;
the artwork remains the copyright of Harvest Records.

HARVEST

LISTENING TO RICHARD BRAUTIGAN

Side One:

The Telephone Door to Richard Brautigan
Trout Fishing in America
Love Poem*
A Confederate General from Big Sur
Here Are the Sounds of My Life in San Francisco
The Pill Versus the Springhill Mine Disaster

Side Two:

Revenge of the Lawn
The Telephone Door That Leads Eventually to Some Love Poems
In Watermelon Sugar
Here Are Some More Sounds of My Life
Short Stories about California
Boo, Forever

*Read by:

Bob Prescott
Valerie Estes   Herb Caen
Michael McClure   Betty Kirkendall
Margot Patterson Doss   Peter Berg
Bruce Conner   Alan Stone
Michaela Blake-Grand   Antonio
Don Allen/David Schaff   Don Allen
Ianthe Brautigan   Cynthia Harwood
Imogen Cunningham   Price Dunn

Recorded at Golden State Recorders in San Francisco
Engineered by Mike Larner
Cover photographs by Edmund Shea

Richard Brautigan has written:

Trout Fishing in America
A Confederate General from Big Sur
In Watermelon Sugar
Please Plant This Book
All Watched Over by Machines of Loving Grace
The Pill Versus the Springhill Mine Disaster
ROMMEL DRIVES ON DEEP INTO EGYPT
etc.

Produced by
MILES ASSOCIATES
and
RICHARD BRAUTIGAN

MANUFACTURED BY CAPITOL RECORDS, INC., A SUBSIDIARY OF CAPITOL INDUSTRIES, INC., HOLLYWOOD AND VINE STREETS, HOLLYWOOD, CALIF. ● FACTORIES: SCRANTON, PA., LOS ANGELES, CALIF., JACKSONVILLE, ILL., WINCHESTER, VA.

GOLDEN STATE RECORDERS, Inc.

665 Harrison Street • San Francisco, California 94107

Area Code 415, 781-6306

PROGRAM	RICHARD BRAUTIGAN	
CLIENT	APPLE RECORDS	
ADDRESS		

STUDIO A	ENG MIKE, VANCE	ORIG RECORDING DATE VARIOUS	W. O. NO:

REEL NO 1	OF: 2	TAPE MCH NO: 4	TAPE SPEED: 15 IPS STEREO	XX	MONAURAL

REMARKS		2 TRK XX	3 TRK	4 TRK

	MASTER NO	TAKE NO.	TITLE	TIME
1	SIDE 1	LDR	CONVERSATION WITH APPLE	.50
2		LDR	HUNCHBACK TROUT	2.09
3		LDR	LOVE POEM	3.34
4		LDR	CONFEDERATE GENERAL IN BIG SUR	4.10
5		LDR	SOUNDS OF MY LIFE	3.22
6		LDR	THE PILL VS. THE SPRINGHILL MINING DISASTER	6.20
7				
8				
9				
10				
11				
12				
13				
14				

REMARKS

MASTERS BY	DATE:	STUDIO:	SEC	ROW	BIN
LPI SIDE #1		LPI SIDE #2	V P C		V D C

GOLDEN STATE RECORDERS, Inc.
665 Harrison Street • San Francisco, California 94107
Area Code 415. 781-6306

PROGRAM	RICHARD BRAUTIGAN						
CLIENT:	APPLE RECORDS						
ADDRESS							

STUDIO	A	ENG MIKE, VANCE	ORIG RECORDING DATE	VARIOUS		W. O. NO.	

REEL NO.	2	OF 2	TAPE MCH NO. 4	TAPE SPEED 15 IPS	STEREO	XX	MONAURAL

REMARKS			2 TRK	XX	3 TRK	4 TRK	

	MASTER NO.	TAKE NO.	TITLE	TIME
1	SIDE 2 2	LDR	REVENGE OF THE LAWN	2.52
2		LDR	~~TELEPHONE RINGS~~	.93
3			TELEPHONE DISCUSSION	.54
4			~~TELEPHONE RINGS~~	1.04
5			~~DISCUSSION OF READING~~	
6			LOVE POEMS	4.46
7		LDR	IN WATERMELON SUGAR	3.22
8		LDR	SOUNDS OF MY LIFE	2.49
9		LDR	SHORT STORIES	6.05
10		LDR	BOO Forever	.42
11				
12				
13				
14				

REMARKS

MASTERS BY	DATE:	STUDIO	SEC	ROW	BIN
LPI SIDE #1		LPI SIDE #2		V.P.C.	V.O.C.

better idea and assembled a group of his friends to read it. So, on the day of the recording, the studio was filled with people: his friend Bob Prescott, the poet Michael McClure (who was a great supporter of Brautigan's work and whom I was also recording), the artist Bruce Conner (who was also the editor of *Semina* magazine), Richard's friends Betty Kirkendall, Margot Patterson Doss and Michaela Blake-Grand, the legendary photographer Imogen Cunningham (who later taught Allen Ginsberg how to take pictures), *San Francisco Chronicle* columnist Herb Caen (who invented the word 'Beatnik'), Peter Berg, Alan Stone, Antonio, Cynthia Harwood and Price Dunn. Valerie Estes read and brought along her old boss, the editor Don Allen who compiled the famous *New American Poetry* anthology. Don Allen read the poem alone and as a duet with David Schaff. Finally Richard's eight-year-old daughter, Ianthe Brautigan, read, and I found out later that Richard paid her $11 for her performance; she spent it all on Cracker Jacks and *Archie* comic books. It was a great session, with everyone milling around in the control booth, waiting their turn.

The other material was straightforward; Richard was a good public speaker, although his deep, slightly cartoonish voice sounded a bit precious at times. However, we rattled through without too many takes. In the end we recorded thirty poems from his book *The Pill Versus the Springhill Mine Disaster*, parts of *A Confederate General from Big Sur*, *Trout Fishing in America* and *In Watermelon Sugar*, and five short stories that were subsequently published in *Revenge of the Lawn: Stories 1962–70*. I left it up to Mike Vance to record the stream and the actual telephone he referred to in the text that were to be used to animate the poems, as getting a lifelike recording of a stream is very technical stuff.

I loved the lifestyle of San Francisco, which was very small-town friendly and a bit cutesy – the population was only about three-quarters of a million and Silicon Valley had not yet been invented.

There was a bohemian atmosphere and a general goodwill among the people, although I perceived a definite pecking order in action among the poets. I was also delighted by the recently introduced FM radio, particularly when Valerie suggested we call up KSAN and make a request. I did, and they immediately played 'Only a Northern Song' by George Harrison, recorded during the *Sgt Pepper* sessions but recently released on the Beatles' *Yellow Submarine* soundtrack. Apple had just sent me a box of new releases, but Valerie's record player was broken. We visited her neighbour, V. Vale, who later became a major force in Beat Generation and counterculture publishing with his *RE/search* series of books, in order to play some of them on his hi-fi.

Golden State Recorders was quite often busy, and so I made use of the time when I was unable to do any recording by asking Valerie to drive around and show me the sights. I got Apple to hire me a car, and we set out over the Golden Gate bridge. We climbed Mount Tamalpais (part-way), and walked among the giant redwoods of Muir Woods, about twelve miles north of San Francisco. We walked on Stinson Beach in the rain and drank in a waterfront bar by the houseboats in Sausalito. It was inevitable that we would have an affair.

So that Richard would not find out, we took several trips back to Los Angeles, where we stayed at the Tropicana Motel on Santa Monica, a home away from home for rock bands. The 'queen-size' bed took up most of the room and the plumbing left a lot to be desired, but it was the Los Angeles equivalent of the famous Hotel Chelsea in New York, where 'anything goes' was the rule. It was on the first trip that we collected the tapes from Charles Bukowski. We drove back up US 1, and I remember spending my birthday in a motel called the Knight's Rest in Pismo Beach, just north of Santa Barbara, overlooking the Pacific. I was falling in love with both Valerie and California.

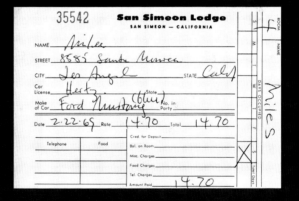

B 005949

RATE $ 11.70 PER: DAY ☑ WK. ☐ MO. ☐

NAME MILES M? 2/

ADDRESS _____

ARRIVAL DATE	ROOM NO.	NO. GUESTS
7/20	207	2
CHANGE		
DATE	TO ROOM	NEW RATE

ITEMS	DATE 7/20	DATE 1/21	DATE 2-22	DATE	DATE	DATE	DATE
BAL. BRO'T. FORWD.			54				
ROOM	11 00	11 00					
ROOM TAX	55	55					
RESTAURANT							
"							
"							
BEVERAGES							
"							
LOCAL TELEPHONE		54					
" "							
LONG DISTANCE							
" "							
" "							
TELEGRAMS							
VALET							
LAUNDRY							
DISBURSEMENTS							
"							
"							
MISCELLANEOUS							
"							
TRANSFERS DR.							
TOTAL CHARGES	11 55	12 09					
PAYMENTS	11 55	11 55	54				
"							
ALLOWANCES							
TRANSFER CR.							
TOTAL CREDITS							
BALANCE DUE	-0-	54					

KAYCO

35542   **San Simeon Lodge**
SAN SIMEON — CALIFORNIA

NAME Miles
STREET 8585 Santa Monica
CITY Los Angeles   STATE Calif
Car License Hertz
Make of Car Ford Mustang (blue)   No. in Party
Date 2-22-69   Rate 14.70   Total 14.70

Telephone	Food

Cred. for Deposit _____
Bal. on Room _____
Misc. Charges _____
Food Charges _____
Tel. Charges _____
Amount Paid 14.70

ROOM / NAME Miles
S M T W T F S

KNIGHTS REST MOTOR LODGE
411 East San Bruno Ave.
San Bruno, California

ROOM	DATE	AMT. PAID	CLERK
16	2/22/69	10.92	

THIS IS YOUR RECEIPT — THANK YOU

Expenses receipts from being on the road with Valerie.

Richard did of course find out, but fortunately I had finished the actual recording process by then. He didn't need to be in the studio for the mix-down from two-inch to quarter-inch tape or the initial sequencing of the material. In keeping with the original concept of Zapple, Richard had complete control over the contents of the album and the cover art. Mike Vance and I made a rough assembly of the album, literally making sure each side was basically the same length and trying to get an interesting dynamic in the order that the tracks were sequenced. I timed all the tracks[3] so that I would know the side lengths when Richard decided upon his final order and arranged for Golden State Recorders to send the tapes directly to Apple in London, rather than to Capitol. I made a 15 ips safety copy of the album to take with me, a normal precaution in any production in case the masters got lost or damaged.

Meanwhile, on 7 March, the slow bureaucracy of Apple's accounts department finally sent Richard a cheque for $200 as an advance on royalties, and Ron Kass promised to send a contract to him in a few days. Meanwhile Richard began working on the sleeve. He wrote and told me, rather pompously, 'The title of the record is going to be *Listening to Richard Brautigan*. It is direct and to the point.' This was something we had already agreed. He continued, 'I like the idea of black and white photographs. I may use two or three photographs on the record, but I am not going to send negatives. I am going to send prints, because the developing is very important and I always like to have it done in a way that pleases me.' He thought the title should be set in a very clear and simple type and that the other text on the sleeve should be in a typeface with the 'same design value'.

Brautigan got his friend Edmund Shea to take the photographs to be used on the cover and for publicity purposes, for which he charged $300 – a huge amount in those days (about three times the average weekly wage). Prints and contact sheets cost extra. In fact this was more than any sleeve had cost so far at Apple (aside from the Beatles'

Valerie Estes, photographed in her apartment, which Miles stayed in while working on the Brautigan album. She was Brautigan's girlfriend at the time of the recording and featured on the cover of Brautigan's album.

Listening to Richard Brautigan -
   Richard Brautigan - Harvest ST-424

567-3389 is Richard Brautigan's telephone
number. He lives in San Francisco and
is over thirty. He writes short novels,
stories, poems and reminiscenses. And he
doesn't always answer the phone.

If you should phone him and it is one of
the times he doesn't always answer the
phone, here are several things you can do
unitl the next time you phone him to see
if it will or won't be one of the times
he doesn't always answer the phone:

   a. read and/or reread; A CONFEDERATE
GENERAL FROM BIG SUR /TROUT FISHING IN
AMERICA/IN WATERMELON ON SUGAR/THE PILL
VERSUS THE SPRINGFIELD MINING DISASTER

   b. make a list of adjectives you will
use when you phone him and it isn't one
of the times he doesn't always answer the
phone: GENTILE/WARM/WEIRD/QUIET/PEACEFUL/
WONDERFUL/BRILLIANT/STRANGE

   c. chances are though that when you
phone him it will be one of those times
he doesn't answer the phone so you will
have to spend your spare time between
phone calls: LISTENING TO RICHARD
BRAUTIGAN/HARVEST ST424

   d. make a list of adjectives you will
use when you phone him and it maybe isn't
one of those times he doesn't answer the
phone: GENTILE/WARM/WEIRD/PEACEFUL/QUIET/
WONDERFUL/BRILLIANT/STRANGE

   e. chances are though that when you
phone him it will be one of those times
he doesn't always answer the phone so you
will have to spend your time between
phone calls rereading and relistening to
CONFEDERATE GENERAL FROM BIG SUR/TROUT
FISHING IN AMERICA/IN WATERMELON SUGAR/
THE PILL VERSUS THE SPRINGFIELD MINING
DISASTER/LISTENING TO RICHARD BRAUTIGAN/
HARVEST ST 424

   f. tell yourself that he is one
GENTILE/WARM/WEIRD/QUIET/PEACEFUL/
WONDERFUL/BRILLIANT/STARNGE
person, even though he doesn't always
answer the phone.

(KHR Volume 2, Issue 2)

KING HARVEST REVIEW

A contemporary review of *Listening to Richard Brautigan*. The allusion
to contacting Richard on the phone evokes the final cover photographs

own records), let alone Zapple, and the photographs weren't even very good. There was muttering from the accounts department, and I can't say I blamed them. Valerie received $50 as a model. I can only assume that Richard did it as a form of revenge for Valerie and me having had an affair, but it was not as if he was monogamous. Golden State sent the tapes but there was a slight problem; a leader tape had come unstuck or something happened and I had to cut about one inch of twisted tape off the 'Sounds of My Life' track and splice the leader back on. For some reason I informed Richard of this, who insisted that a new copy of the tape be used. 'I am very interested in the timing of that track and want it just the way we recorded it in San Francisco.'[4] Golden State subsequently airmailed a new copy from the USA. As one inch of 15 ips tape – fifteen inches per second – amounted to only one-fifteenth of a second, an inaudible amount, and as the new tape would be second generation, rather than the master, I ignored this instruction. It mattered little, anyway, because by then the fragmentation of Apple, and consequently of Zapple, had already begun.

I loved the lifestyle of San Francisco, which was very small-town friendly and a bit cutesy . . . There was a bohemian atmosphere and a general goodwill among the people, although I perceived a definite pecking order in action among the poets.

Chapter 11

The First Trip:
SF - Ferlinghetti - McClure

Lawrence Ferlinghetti at Golden State Recorders. None of the tracks recorded there were wasted, but the original album was never released as Miles and Ferlinghetti planned it. Ferlinghetti is also pictured on p. 173 outside the Royal Albert Hall heading to the press conference for the International Poetry Incarnation in 1965.

The First Trip:
SF - Ferlinghetti - McClure

L AWRENCE FERLINGHETTI WAS ONE of the Beat Generation poets I most admired. When I was at art college in Stroud, Gloucestershire, in 1961, we painted his long poem 'Dog' on the wall of the living-room of the medieval house that I and a group of artists lived in. It was taken from *A Coney Island of the Mind,* one of my favourite books. I met him in 1965 when he arrived in London to stay with Julie Felix, the American folk singer who was making a name for herself as Britain's answer to Joan Baez – she had the same high clear voice and, for that matter, the same long straight hair, only lighter. I produced and released a spoken-word album, *Lawrence Ferlinghetti at Better Books,* of him reading his poems at the bookshop in the summer of 1965, which included a musical accompaniment by Julie Felix on one of the tracks, recorded at her apartment in Chelsea. He was one of the stars of the Royal Albert Hall poetry reading that summer; his poem 'To Fuck Is to Love Again' causing a commotion with the aged attendants, one of whom I overheard mutter to another, 'He's yelling "Fuck!" at them and they're loving it!' shaking his head in astonishment. Ferlinghetti's poetry was written with public performance in mind, and he had in fact made an album of himself reading his poems to a jazz backing that was released on Fantasy back in 1957.

Allen Ginsberg had been staying with me in London during summer 1965, at the end of which visit he and Ferlinghetti left for Paris. But Lawrence had enjoyed himself so much in London that he decided to return for a final ten days and came to stay in the spare bed in my study that Allen had recently vacated. Lawrence was tall, casual, slow-moving and slow-talking, with intense blue eyes – the eyes of a poet – and an easy smile but a mouth that could at times look cruel. He had strong, fiercely defended values – for instance he was opposed to arts patronage by governments, thinking that it was certain to compromise artists' freedom and integrity. He was an early environmentalist, a peace activist, an old-time anarchist and in every sense a bohemian. He owned and ran the City Lights bookshop on Columbus Avenue in San Francisco and was the publisher of City Lights Books, a small literary press specializing in modern poetry. In 1956 he published *Howl and Other Poems*, putting Allen Ginsberg, and City Lights, on the map by being prosecuted for obscenity. I liked Lawrence very much and knew that it would not take long to record an album with him because he had done so many poetry readings and knew just how to deliver his poems.

In San Francisco I met him at his famous bookshop, City Lights, at 261 Columbus Avenue. I had sent $2 away to this address in 1960 for copies of *On the Road*, *The Dharma Bums* and *Howl*, so it was a great pleasure finally to see the building. We also discussed the album at his house on Francisco Street. One of the pleasures of this kind of trip was to see people's homes and get an inkling of how they lived.

I really enjoyed recording 'Assassination Raga' and the poem 'Moscow in the Wilderness, Segovia in the Snow', where Lawrence brought in a very accomplished guitarist, Jeffrey Chinn, to accompany him. Some of his works were written as songs, others were written to be funny, such as 'I Asked Krishnamurti for His Autograph' which we had to record over and over again because it kept getting too serious. Lawrence was a real pro.

The other album I hoped to record in San Francisco was by Michael McClure, whose 'Lion' poem I had already remastered before heading out to America. Michael had been in London prior to my leaving for the opening of his play *The Beard*, and we had discussed his album. My original idea was to include some of his

This photograph was intended as the background for a 'Blue Note' style album
sleeve for Ferlinghetti's album with the name of the artist and title of the album to be
superimposed on it in colour. The photograph shows a huge crowd gathered in

'Beast Language'; I am a great fan of 'sound poetry', like that of Schwitters and Ernst Jandl, and thought that Zapple buyers would enjoy this explosive, yet carefully nuanced new language. However, since McClure's return to San Francisco, he had changed his mind about what he wanted to do and seemed to see the record as a chance to become a pop star on the Beatles' label. Michael was still in his thirties, handsome, with a twinkle in his eye. He drove a Harley Davidson chopper and hung out with Hells Angels; he dressed in leather like his friend Jim Morrison. He knew Dylan and wrote Janis Joplin's 'Oh Lord, Won't You Buy Me a Mercedes Benz' for her, recorded three days before she died. I once described him as 'the Prince of San Francisco', with his Byronic good looks, fine head of hair, his acclaimed poetry and plays and his easy way with women. In 1967 he published *Freewheelin' Frank*, the biography of Frank Reynolds of the Hells Angels as dictated to him, and now he decided that he wanted to share the album with Frank.

Freewheelin' Frank was a man of strong beliefs and great loyalty; you felt that he would be a good friend to have – and not just because of his colours. Michael wanted to make music with him, un-rehearsed, spontaneous music. 'Let's do some numbers!' he said. 'Why not?' I replied, interested to see what would come out of it but worried about the cost. We recorded a lot of music, with Frank on harmonica and tambourine and Michael playing the autoharp, which had been given to him by Bob Dylan. We recorded a long lop-ing tune called 'The Allen Ginsberg for President Waltz', in not quite waltz time, then Frank read some of his poetry: 'Hymn to Lucifer', during which Michael played a strange, scraping, Eastern instrument that no one knew the name of. Mike, the engineer, was not too happy about the way they kept wandering off microphone, but on playback those fades actually worked very well. The problem was that the album, as yet, had no focus. The studio staff were also somewhat upset by the fact that Frank insisted on parking his chopper right in the middle of the studio, instead of discreetly at the side out of the way. No one wanted to knock the thing over. I liked Frank, and he even gave me a signed copy of his poems, but I couldn't see an album coming out of these sessions.

It looked as if we were wasting our time, so I took Michael for a walk and tried to explain that the studio was costing $3 a minute and that he should come back when we had discussed something more concrete and usable. We walked down to the bay and back, and Michael told me that this was the first time he had actually listened to anyone in years. He recognized that he was narcissistic and that his success had insulated him from much of everyday reality. He resolved to focus on the album and come back with some solid ideas, maybe just reading his poetry or acting one of his short plays. Fortunately there had been other things for Mike Vance to do in the studio while we were gone, otherwise it would have been an expensive walk.

He had strong, fiercely defended
values . . . He was an early
environmentalist, a peace
activist, an old-time anarchist
and in every sense a bohemian.

Chapter 12

Back in Blighty

George Harrison photographed outside his home following the police raiding his house for drugs on the day of Paul McCartney's wedding to Linda.

Back in Blighty

EMBOLDENED BY HIS SUCCESS in busting John and Yoko, Detective Sergeant Norman Pilcher, who had a personal vendetta against pop stars, now vindictively chose Paul McCartney's wedding day, 12 March 1969, to raid George Harrison's house. Pilcher, who was well known for planting evidence, 'found' a block of hash in a shoe, provoking George Harrison's memorable comment: 'I'm a tidy person, I keep my socks in the sock drawer and my hash in the hash box. It's not mine.' George telephoned Release, the 24-hour emergency assistance service charity set up by Caroline Coon to help people arrested on drug charges. Release was probably the most important of all the underground, hippie organizations and finished up handling a third of all drug cases in Britain. Release quickly found him an appropriate lawyer who was able to help. As the outcome of George's case was successful – George and Pattie were each fined £250 plus 10 guineas costs – Caroline asked Derek Taylor if it was possible to set up a meeting with George in the hope that he would make a contribution towards the enormous costs of their tremendous workload, the lawyers' fees and court appearances. She wanted to submit a formal appeal for funds. Peter Asher and I attended the meeting in George's office. It was friendly, with George in a happy mood, and culminated in George opening the drawer in his desk and producing his chequebook. He filled one in, folded it over and handed it to Caroline. She thanked him profusely, expecting something like £50, but was too polite to look and see how much it was until I had accompanied her to the front door. She was gobsmacked – it was for £5,000, enough for Release to buy the building next door to their office on Princedale Road and move from their cramped, rented rooms to something much more spacious. A photocopy of George's cheque hung on the wall of Release for many years. I thought George was particularly generous and was very pleased with the outcome. As for Pilcher, he was eventually charged with conspiracy to pervert the course of justice, and, although he had cannily resigned from the police before his case came to court, his attempt to escape justice by emigrating to Australia failed. On arrival in Freemantle he was extradited straight back to Britain where, in September 1973, he was sentenced to four years in gaol.

George Harrison's and John's and Yoko's albums were still to be released on 9 May – but by now everyone was dragging their feet about the other releases. The first one being the Ken Kesey album. Recriminations flew around the building; questions were asked about who commissioned it in the first place. It certainly wasn't me; Kesey was never on my list. It probably came up in a conversation between Paul McCartney and Derek Taylor, with some mention made of the role that Kesey's Merry Pranksters and their psychedelic bus had in the origins of the *Magical Mystery Tour* film. The problem was that Kesey was now associated with the Hells Angels and the trouble Apple had in getting rid of them. He was, as they say, 'on the elbow list'.

My office at Apple was at the top, next to Peter Asher's, but as Ken Kesey had absconded with my Revox I couldn't do any actual editing there, although I did borrow a machine for basic playbacks. However, I was able to prepare both the Brautigan and Ferlinghetti albums for release as there was no further editing to do on them; all I needed were the sleeve illustrations and the cover copy. I did a rough edit of the McClure album, taking out all the false starts and fluffs and reducing it to the basic material we would use. I made further contact with Kenneth Rexroth and Kenneth Patchen, both of whom were interested in releasing albums. By then we had also come up with a plan for a set of signed limited editions of the albums, with sleeves on thicker cardboard and with inserts which would not appear on the regular issues containing unpublished poems or texts as well as a signature. This would give extra money to the artists and help pay for the Zapple series. My studio costs alone were already more than $4,000.

In his wonderful autobiography, *The Longest Cocktail Party*, Richard DiLello often sums up the state of affairs at Apple at the time with fictitious, but authentic, passages of dialogue, quoting conversations between two unnamed protagonists which frequently sound like him and Derek Taylor. In a section set at the end of April 1969, he comments that Peter Asher says that the Richard Brautigan album is all ready to go; he adds that nothing can happen until the contract has been finalized and that the pressings and the printing of the sleeve were not getting the go-ahead until that had happened. 'I've got a feeling that that one is going to be on ice now that the new regime has begun. It's probably going to die a slow death and Richard Brautigan will never walk through that white door downstairs.'[1] This sounds like Derek, and the new regime, of course, referred to the fact that on 21 March 1969 Allen Klein was appointed business manager of Apple.

The Brautigan sleeve was indeed done and ready to go. It featured two photographs: one of Richard holding a telephone and another of Valerie, outside her place on Kearney, also holding a telephone. All of Richard's previous books had shown him with his latest girlfriend. The use of two pictures was perhaps symbolic of the growing rift between them. The release date was set for 23 May 1969.

Richard DiLello also comments in this part of his book that Paul's original design for the series will not now be used and that both George and John and Yoko had done their own sleeves for their albums. Paul's original idea, to unite the whole series of Zapple albums and make them more collectable, was to have an outer sleeve with a large apple cut out of it, so that the actual album sleeve showed through. This, however, was deemed unacceptable to record retailers who knew that the cut-out would get damaged and torn, leading to many returns, so it was rejected.

Pilcher, who was well known for planting evidence, 'found' a block of hash in a shoe, provoking George Harrison's memorable comment: 'I'm a tidy person, I keep my socks in the sock drawer and my hash in the hash box. It's not mine.'

Chapter 13

Unfinished Music No. 2:
Life with the Lions

John and Yoko performing at Lady Mitchell Hall; John is sitting
cross-legged on the stage with his back to the audience.
This performance became side one of *Life with the Lions*.

Unfinished Music No. 2: Life with the Lions

W E RELEASED ZAPPLE 01, *Unfinished Music No. 2: Life with the Lions*, on 9 May 1969. It certainly lived up to Zapple's claim to release unusual experimental sounds, although the public had been prepared for it by the release of *Unfinished Music No. 1: Two Virgins*, the year before and all the unfavourable critical attention that was heaped on it. *Life with the Lions* was just as uncompromising. The title was a play on words, similar to the old Beatles titles, like *Revolver* (something which revolves, also a gun) or *Rubber Soul* (white soul music or the sole of a tennis shoe or sneaker). In this instance it was a play on the name of a BBC radio and (later) television domestic sitcom *Life with the Lyons* that ran from 1950 to 1951 on radio and then for five seasons, from 1955 to 1960, on television. It featured a real American family, actor Ben Lyon and his wife, the actress Bebe Daniels (who had moved to London during the war, where they featured in the BBC radio series *Hi Gang!* with Vic Oliver that ran from 1940 to 1949). *Life with the Lyons* also starred their children, Richard and Barbara Lyon, and was hugely popular for its naturalism; it was scripted, but it reflected and expanded upon real events of the time. Lennon would have grown up with it.

Lennon described *Unfinished Music* as 'It is saying whatever you want it to say. It is just us expressing ourselves like a child does, you know, however he feels like then. What we're saying is make your own music. This is Unfinished Music.'[1]

Side one was taken up by one long track: 'Cambridge 1969'. On a quiet Sunday afternoon on 2 March 1969, at Cambridge University's Lady Mitchell Hall, Yoko Ono, accompanied by John

Lennon, performed as part of a concert of experimental music before an audience of five hundred students. She had been invited some time before in her position as a Fluxus artist who had appeared with John Cage, Ornette Coleman and other new music composers and performers. The organizers did not know that she and Lennon were together, and his appearance was not expected. The organizer, Anthony Barnett, asked her if she was going to bring a band or accompaniment. Yoko asked John what he thought and he told her, 'Well, I'm the band, but don't tell them, you know. I'll be the band.' So she told him, 'Yes, I'll bring a band with me.'

Lennon had very ambivalent feelings about anything avant-garde and had come up with the memorable phrase 'Avant-garde is French for bullshit'. He was deeply suspicious of anything that he couldn't understand or that was above his head intellectually and put it down mercilessly in interviews and conversation. He told Andy Peebles in a BBC radio interview:

John: We arrived in Cambridge, it was supposed to be an avant-garde – that word again – jazz thing, right. And there was a guy called John Tchicai who was apparently a famous avant-garde sax guy or jazz sax guy – I didn't know any of them. A few people that I don't remember the names of; they were there too. And I turned up as her band, you know. And the people were looking and saying, 'Is it? Is it?' You know. I just had a guitar and an amp and that was the first time I'd played that style, just pure feedback and whatever it is on that track. And the audience were very weird, because they were all these sort of intellectual artsy-fartsies from Cambridge, you know, and they were uptight because the rock-'n'-roll guy was there, even though I wasn't doing any rhythm. If you hear it, it's just pure sound. Because what else can you do when a woman's howling, you know, you just go along with it, right?

Yoko: They were totally solid, you know, very polite.

John: They were totally solid. Well, the reaction I got from the 'quotes, unquotes' avant-garde group – not only in Cambridge – it was the same reaction that she got from the rock-'n'-roll people, like, 'What's she doing here?' Well, when I was doing the stuff with her, this little tight-knit avant-garde scene would be saying, 'What the hell . . . who the hell is he? He's one of those pop . . .' So we're both getting schtick for not being in the right bag.

Yoko: Do you think they noticed . . . do you think they noticed, because I mean . . .?

John: You bet they noticed. They were trying so hard not to notice. You know that when you go in a restaurant. You can always tell people are trying not to look at you. You know, they're being cool, and you pick up this sort of vibe, or whatever you call it, coming from people not looking at you, you know. It's worse than when they look.[2]

In fact Douglas Oliver, in the *Cambridge Evening News,* gave a neutral report of the event, sounding as if they didn't really know what to make of it – a view shared by many others – but were doing their best:

> Miss Ono began with a fearsome siren note, as Japanese as a Noh Play Chant, and sustained it to the point of self-torture. Lennon was squatting at her feet, back to the audience, holding, shaking, swinging electric guitars right up against a large speaker, or hitting the instrument against the speaker, to create ear-splitting feedbacks . . . The concert was strange and chilling, not in a bad sense, but because so much unusual sound texture and harsh melody were disturbing. At no time did the music become comforting. It was an extraordinary experience.[3]

Yoko, with John, had the opening set, followed after a break by a group of well-known free jazz musicians including saxophonist John Tchicai and percussionist John Stevens. It was Yoko's show; she howled and screeched at the front of the stage while John sat at the back in the shadows and accompanied her on an over-loud feedback guitar. The organizer, Anthony Barnett, said, 'Lennon had been trying to show off and be more avant-garde than anyone in avant-garde music.' John and Yoko had told the other musicians, 'If you would like to join us for some improvisation, please do.' At the very end they were joined onstage by John Tchicai and John Stevens.

John Tchicai, the Danish free saxophonist and composer (1936–2012), had played with John Coltrane and Albert Ayler as a sideman. He was a member of Archie Shepp's New York Contemporary Five and led the New York Art Quartet. Critic Mort Maizlish described him: 'Tchicai plays in a dry, metallic manner that at first makes other styles appear florid. He is, however, an extremely inventive and emotional player, whose tonal innovations do not follow even the conventions of "originality".'[4] John Stevens, at that time less well known, was a free-improvisation English drummer (1940–94) and a founding member of the Spontaneous Music Ensemble. They had their own audience and group of followers; the appearance of John Lennon would not have been greeted with derision, just puzzlement. It was only the second time Lennon had played apart from the other members of the Beatles, and, as Lennon himself said, it was the first time he had ever tried to play feedback guitar. He did not have the control of Pete Townshend or Jimi Hendrix, nor did he have the skill of the many free jazz players who used feedback as part of their performance, so any criticism – if indeed there was any – was probably valid.

Lennon's ambivalence towards avant-garde music was not something he ever really resolved: he was unfamiliar with the developments in modern music and in free jazz, and so he dismissed them all out of hand as 'intellectual crap'. However, this was the background that Yoko came from: she had played with John Cage and others and had recently collaborated with Ornette Coleman in an evening of experimental music at the Royal Albert Hall. This particular evening seems to have been the cause of a certain amount of jealousy on John's part, and it was interesting to see how he came to terms with it. The event had by then turned into something of a *cause célèbre*: first of all the British Musicians' Union would not allow Ornette to play unless a British musician was offered a similar gig in America (an absurd restriction that set British jazz back by decades because virtually none of the new American musicians were able to play in the UK, and the UK had no players of international status to exchange). Ornette eventually was allowed to come over from Paris, where he was living, after a campaign to get music professors all over Britain to write in claiming he was a *classical* musician. That worked, and the concert was scheduled for 29 February 1968. Ornette brought with him the same sidemen he used earlier that month in Milan, an unusual combination utilizing the twinned basses of David Izenson and Charlie Haden, along with Edward Blackwell on drums.

Trouble arose almost immediately at rehearsals because Ornette's sidemen were unable to understand Yoko's directions; they were too abstract and poetic to give any clear musical instruction. Coleman suggested that she write it down, but this did not help much as the text was a typical piece of baffling, whimsical and somewhat erotic Yoko poetry. The musicians liked it and suggested that it be used in the programme, even though it could not be used as a guide to her intentions. The programme was printed, but when the Albert Hall officials saw it they regarded it as obscene – Yoko's instructions included words like 'shit' and 'penis', and the programmes were all confiscated and destroyed. Yoko had more produced which were handed out on the night with the tickets, but even then the guards

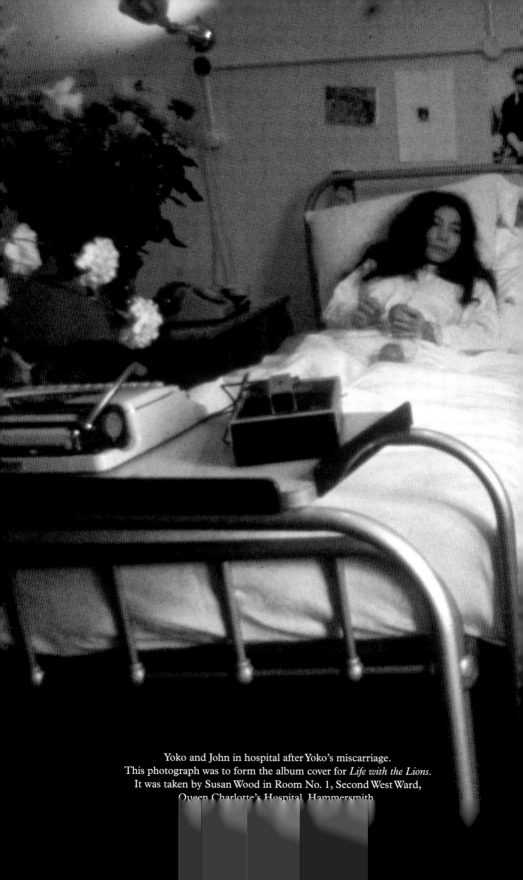

Yoko and John in hospital after Yoko's miscarriage.
This photograph was to form the album cover for *Life with the Lions*.
It was taken by Susan Wood in Room No. 1, Second West Ward,
Queen Charlotte's Hospital, Hammersmith.

attempted to confiscate them, in some cases grabbing them from the hands of people who had already paid for them. The hall then ordered a stop to the sale of tickets, but this caused a near riot, with the crowd outside chanting, 'Let the people in! Let the people in!' So rather than have to call the police, the hall relented and allowed the concert to proceed. The concert itself did have a somewhat sexual theme, with Yoko's cries and grunts sounding like sexual intercourse, as Ornette and the trio provided suitable honks and squeals.

That September I spoke with Lennon about the Ornette concert, as well as his recent concert in Toronto with the Plastic Ono Band: a pick-up band consisting of Eric Clapton, bassist Klaus Voorman and drummer Alan White. We also talked about the Cambridge concert with Yoko, which was included on *Unfinished Music No. 2: Life with the Lions* that had been released four months earlier. At that time all conversations and interviews in John's and Yoko's front room on the ground floor of Apple were being tape-recorded.[5] In this section of the transcript John is talking about the Plastic Ono Band's appearance at the Toronto Rock-'n'-Roll Revival on 13 September, ten days earlier:

John: You'd have enjoyed it . . . It was really something; it finally happened that night – something happened on stage all right, and in the crowd. Because we didn't know what we were going to do, a rock-'n'-roll audience, and how the reaction would be. But something magical happened that night. The fact that it affected Eric and Klaus and Alan – they really got turned on by that experience. So that turned us on even more. The whole thing really just was a big, big turn-on. And it was like a new direction. We didn't do anything we didn't do at Cambridge, or that Yoko hadn't really done with Ornette Coleman at Albert Hall. But the fact [is] that when she first gave me her Albert Hall stuff I grooved to it. I was saying all that intellectual jazz, but going on in the background, 'Can't stand it. Can't stand it! Let's do it together, do it this way.' Conceptually you think you're going to howl and the musician's going to play, but the difference between Ornette Coleman intellectualizing that jazz, which is just, to me, intellectual literary crap coming out of a trumpet or whatever he plays, and just playing rock 'n' roll, or just playing the amplifier, is tremendous, you know, and that's what happened in Cambridge because it was small, it was a small experience.

Yoko: And that happened too because I didn't need John then. I was going through a phase of all that scene when I was the oddball because my thing was that I was less theoretical than most of them. I was intuitive, and so when I followed even, say, Ornette, you can obviously see immediately that Ornette's job is highly intellectualized, sophisticated stuff. And I'm howling, and the combination is not a combination really; it's not merging, it's sort of separate. But I didn't have anybody else to merge with. But then I met John who was having the same kind of problem. He was always having to cut himself down for the Beatles and playing old stuff by himself at home. He was really freaking out at home. And I've heard some of that freaked-out stuff that he did at home. I really wanted to groove, you know. And this time it was really very easy, because both of us are basically intuitive people and we are normal oddballs. And you know what they say, when two people dream it's a reality. We were like in a dream state, and then he came and we started to make love.

John: I've never heard any avant-garde stuff that I'd wanna bring in. I'd sooner have ten Eric Claptons. I'd sooner get a Salvation Army Band than get a lot of avant-garde people to squeak and play all that intellectual crap. I think anything's valid, but if Yoko says this is a particular performer that I recommend and we should perform with him, then I'd do it, but anything I've heard has always left me cold. I haven't heard anything better than a car engine yet . . .

It's just like if I painted myself blue. What could we do about it? If there's a concert on and for my turn of the party I want to be painted blue there's nothing to intellectualize about . . . I mean, some of the letters from the kids, they're having no trouble [with what I do]. Sixty thousand kids in America are having no trouble with *Life with the Lions*. I mean, there's always going to be people complaining because we left the Cavern and went to work in Manchester, you know. That's all it is really. How dare I leave the Cavern and jump in a white bag in the Albert Hall? But I can't wait around for those people to decide they'd like me to go into tap dancing.

If the Beatles had just gone into showbiz, there would have been nothing said; we would have got probably a knighthood and nothing but praise, but we're not looking for that. At least I'm not, and so I must just do what I want, and I can't. It's like we couldn't take a poll at the Cavern to see if they thought it was suitable for John Lennon, Paul, George and Ringo to go and play in Croydon because the poll would have said, 'No, stay at home', and we couldn't have taken a poll as to whether the Beatles went to America or not because most of the British fans would have said, 'No, stay here', you know, and it's only the same thing going on. I'm just moving out, or pressing the outer limits of whatever's going on and people say, 'How dare you, I don't understand why you're leaving your cosy rut and doing something else? Why don't you stay in your rut where we can recognize you?' There's no time for waiting for people to understand why I've grown a beard or why I've shaved it off, or why I want to be naked or why I want to stand on my head; there's no time for it. You know, if people waited for people to understand everything they did, nothing would ever be done.

I'm not a politician so I don't rely on public taste or public opinion as to how I run my life. I refuse to do that. I mean, I don't even consider it. For a politician to go into a white bag in the Albert Hall he'd have to consider the effects it would have on his constituents, but I'm not a politician, and I don't owe my constituents anything other than I create something, whatever it is, and they accept it or reject it on its own merits and not on any preconceived ideas.

The second side of *Life with the Lions* was composed of cassette recordings made in Room 1, Second Ward West, Queen Charlotte's Hospital, between 4 and 25 November 1968, the world-renowned maternity hospital on Du Cane Road, London W12, that Yoko had been admitted to following complications with her pregnancy.

Track one, 'No Bed for Beatle John', is John and Yoko chanting the texts of press cuttings a cappella style: these include a report that John had no bed to stay in overnight and had to sleep on the floor and of how EMI refused to distribute *Unfinished Music No. 1: Two Virgins* because of its controversial cover showing them both naked. Lennon said, 'On "No Bed for Beatle John", it's another diary of how we are now. We just thought it would be nice to sing these press cuttings because they're stylized and people just read them out usually. We chose them because it is what people were saying about us in that [hospital] room. We never left that room to make that record. We even made a film while we were in that room. We were reading about ourselves like everybody else reads about us. So, we thought about singing it'.[6]

The second track, 'Baby's Heartbeat', is a recording of the actual heartbeat of their baby, John Ono Lennon II, recorded using a Nagra microphone and looped to last four minutes.

Track three, 'Two Minutes Silence', can be seen as a memorial to their son, who miscarried shortly after the recording was made, and can also be read as a reference to John Cage's famous '4'33"', which requires listening to the relative silence of a room for that length of time, although John's and Yoko's silence is just dead tape.

The last track is 'Radio Play', a collage of John and Yoko in conversation, Lennon making a telephone call and snatches of the sounds of a radio. An edited version of this track was first released as a flexi-record and included in an issue of *Aspen*, the art magazine that appeared in a box.

A month earlier Detective Sergeant Norman Pilcher and his Drugs Squad team had raided Montagu Square. John and Yoko always maintained that Yoko's miscarriage was brought on by the stress of the raid. The front sleeve of the album is a photograph, taken by Susan Wood, of Yoko in bed with John on his mattress on the floor at Queen Charlotte's where Yoko was recovering. The hospital did not have enough beds, and so John had to bed down on a mattress on the floor.

The back-cover news agency photograph shows the distraught and scared-looking couple leaving Marylebone Magistrates' Court on 19 October, the day after the police raid on Montagu Square. The back cover also carried a quote from George Martin, the Beatles' producer, saying, 'No comment'.

Years later, when asked about the photograph on the sleeve of *Life with the Lions*, showing her in bed in hospital, Yoko was remarkably casual about it:

Yoko Ono: Yes. We had a miscarriage or something, didn't we?
John Lennon: You had a miscarriage, and I was there, the actual reality of it.
Yoko: That's right, exactly . . . We had many miscarriages.
John: We did.
Yoko: Yes, about three.
John: Yeah, enough to make us miserable about it, you know.[7]

The organizers did not know that
she and Lennon were together, and
his appearance was not expected.
The organizer, Anthony Barnett,
asked her if she was going to bring
a band or accompaniment. Yoko asked
John what he thought and he told
her, 'Well, I'm the band, but don't
tell them, you know. I'll be the
band.' So she told him, 'Yes, I'll
bring a band with me.'

Chapter 14

Electronic Sound

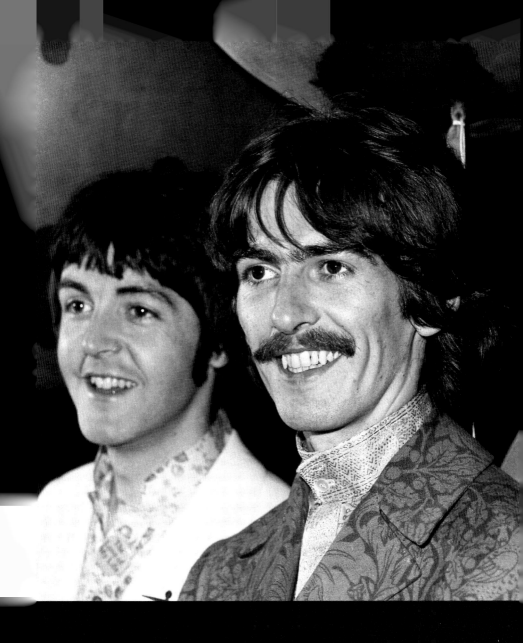

George Harrison with Paul McCartney in 1967. Although Paul seemed to show more interest in the electronic music scene initially, it was George who would release the *Electronic Sound* album, showcasing his experiments with the Moog synthesizer

Electronic Sound

ALTHOUGH I NEVER TALKED with George Harrison about electronic music as such, I know it was one of the areas that interested him and that it was a subject the Beatles discussed between themselves and with George Martin, their producer. Back in December 1966 I had a taped conversation with Paul McCartney in which we predicted that this would be the area that popular music developed into, although neither of us could of course predict Kraftwerk and the rise of techno. Paul said:

> This is the gap in electronics, the one where people, quite a few people, that are prepared for the next sound, they're ready, they're waiting for the next scene in music, the next scene in sound. A lot of people now are ready to be led to the next move. The next move seems to be things like electronics because it just is a different field, it's a complete new field, and there's a lot of good new sounds to be listened to in it. But if the music itself is just going to jump about five miles ahead, then everyone's going to be left standing with this gap of five miles that they've got to all cross before they can even see what scene these people are on and, for instance, with the people . . . I can see that it is in a way a progression to accept random things as being planned. Random is planned, as well, but most people won't accept that and they'd need a lead into it, to accepting that. You can't just say to somebody, 'That machine plays random notes, but it's planned and I can control the amount of random in it.' They'll say, 'What for? Why don't you write a nice tune or why don't you just write some interesting sounds?' That's what I'd like to do. I'd like to look into that gap a bit.

It turned out that George, not Paul, was the first Beatle to investigate it enough to release an album of his experiments when he made *Electronic Sound* two years later. In the meantime, we had all been listening to a lot of electronic music. It was popularized by *Switched On Bach* by Walter (later Wendy) Carlos with Benjamin Folkman, released in September 1968, and was the number ten top American LP of 1969 and stayed in the 'classical' chart for 310 weeks; it was soulless though. Indica Books did import some records, and in my role of 'purveyor of anything hip that you think we should have' to the Beatles, I had sent them all copies of *Silver Apples of the Moon* by Morton Subotnik (1968), who worked with a modular voltage-controlled synthesizer, which he called the Electric Music Box. It seemed the sort of thing they would all want to hear. (Other records I sent to them all included *Freak Out* by the Mothers of Invention, USA edition; *The Heliocentric Worlds of Sun Ra*, volumes one and two; *Ghosts* by Albert Ayler; and *The Fugs* on ESP. Other electronic compositions I sent round were *Philomel* by Milton Babbitt and *Visage* by Luciano Berio.)

The press release accompanying the release of the first two Zapple albums on 9 May 1969 described the label:

Zapple is . . . an extension of everything raw and different which Apple has tried to bring to the record business. On Zapple you will hear eccentricities . . . Zapple will bring sounds of all kinds . . . not necessarily music as you know it, love it or fear it. There will be electronic sounds, spoken-word, recorded interviews . . . We may . . . and whisper it with infinite subtlety, only loud enough so that it may be heard, no louder . . . have some classical music.

However imaginative he was, when it came down to it, Derek Taylor had not the faintest idea how to promote George's *Electronic Sound* album; he just couldn't find an angle that would interest the *Daily Mirror* or the *Express*. He aimed instead at the underground press, also hoping that some of the Fleet Street hacks would regard themselves as 'switched on' (as the *Mirror* called it) and groove to the freaky new sounds. Then again, he might have just smoked too much hash before he wrote it. His press release, more prose-poem, read:

Zapple
Electronic Sound by George Harrison – Zapple 02

Under the Mersey Wall: side one

In February 1969 in a mounting wortex of decibels
There came to pass a wrecked chord of
Environmental sounds that went beyond the genre
Of hashish cocktail music . . .
The bass line has been milked through the Moog machine
And lo and high we behold electronic music . . . music
That becomes sounds that are food for the mind,
Not to forget the soul, o sole mio.
Dear George, would you be so kind
And fulfil this request
And play the lost chord
The one I like best.

Under the Mersey Wall/science fictionalized horrors
Of man in his lyrical home grown simplicity.
A wind blew in Esher.

No Time or Space: side two

In California through the machine gun of his mind George
Thought aloud to himself and in his composure he has
Exposed the thought patterns beating on his brow and
Diametrically opposed he has exposed through the medium
Of the Moog, a pottage of space music. And on and on we go . . .
George Harrison versus Godzilla and King Kong
In space and Bernie Crause [*sic*] was there to give a helping
hand.
Dear George, say hi to Bernie.

The sleeve reproduced two naïve paintings by George made specifically for the album. The front featured a painting of Bernie
Krause, with an inexplicable green face, wearing a bow tie and a
pocket handkerchief, patching in the four modules from which the
sound was synthesized through the sound board of the Moog. The
resulting sounds could be seen pouring out of a large pipe on the
bottom right-hand corner of the sleeve – the 'Trippy Meat Grinder'.
At the bottom centre is a small blue face – Harrison himself – who
says he was making the tea – a white tea set on a folding table is to
the left of the board. His cat, Jostick (*sic*), is the small green-and-
white figure near where the music pours from the spout.
The back sleeve depicts Derek Taylor's press office at Apple with
Derek himself in his huge high-backed wicker chair and described

by George's son Dhani as 'holding on to all of Apple's aggravation and problems' that appear as an angry Japanese kite hovering over everyone.[1] The two faces on the chair-back are Neil Aspinall, frowning, with all the cares of Apple on his shoulders, and Mal Evans, smiling, ever amiable. To the right of the sleeve stands Eric Clapton in full psychedelic mode, complete with permed Jimi Hendrix afro hair. To the left of Derek's chair are the four framed photographs of the Beatles from the *White Album*. At the top left is a lotus-seated yogi with an 'Om' sign above him, only the picture is hung upside down, as is the crude landscape (or window) at the upper right-hand corner.

George's less than convinced approach to anything avant-garde was expressed in two epigrams:

> It could be called avant-garde, but a more apt description would be (in the words of my old friend Alvin) 'Avant-garde clue'!
>
> George Harrison

> There are a lot of people around, making a lot of noise, here's some more.
>
> Arthur Wax

The album consists of two long pieces, one each side. Side one, 'Under the Mersey Wall' (which was inadvertently pressed as side two in the American release with the consequent wrong title), was recorded at George's Los Angeles-style house in Esher, Surrey (London's stockbroker belt), in February 1969. The title is a pun on the regular column, *Over the Mersey Wall*, in the *Liverpool Echo* written by his namesake – no relation – George Harrison, who covered all the early Beatles tours. George is quoted as saying, 'All I did was get that very first Moog synthesizer with the big patch unit and keyboards you could never tune, and I put a microphone into a tape machine. Whatever came out when I fiddled with the knobs went on tape.'[2]

Side two, 'No Time or Space', was recorded in November 1968 at Armin Steiner's Sound Recorders on the corner of Argyle and Yucca in Los Angeles where George was producing the *Is This What You Want?* album with newly signed Apple artist Jackie Lomax. The latest in studio gadgets was the Moog synthesizer, which had been demonstrated at the Monterey Pop Festival in June 1967 by composer-musicians Paul Beaver and Bernie Krause, and had been talked about excitedly by musicians and studio technicians ever since. This cumbersome machine, which resembled an old-fashioned telephone exchange, could not only imitate existing instruments but also create new sounds. George decided that he wanted to use one on the Jackie Lomax album and hired Bernie Krause to play on the session, so on the evening of 11 November Krause brought a Moog III over to Sound Recorders. It was an immensely complicated machine to use, but George was intrigued by it and asked Krause to stay on after the session and demonstrate how he had achieved the sounds he used on the session.

Krause had flown into Los Angeles early that morning from San Francisco, and it was now 3 a.m. and he was exhausted. None the less, he put the machine through its paces, but he hadn't noticed that George had asked the tape operator to keep the tape rolling. Krause wrote in his autobiography, *Into a Wild Sanctuary*, 'Had I been aware that he was recording my demonstration, I would never have shown examples of what Paul [Beaver] and I were considering for our next album, which was to be *Gandharva*. As I showed him the settings and gave some performance examples, Harrison seemed impressed with the possibilities.'[3]

George decided he must have one and asked Krause, who represented the Moog Corporation, when he could have one delivered to London. Bernie told him that like anyone else he could have it thirty days after he received a 50 per cent deposit and it had cleared the bank. George immediately attempted to pull rank, reminding Krause that he was a Beatle and that Apple generally did not make deposits. Bernie was unmoved and repeated the terms, 'in a calm voice and looking him straight in the eye', telling George there were no exceptions; when the cheque cleared his synthesizer would be on its way within a month.

A couple of months later Krause received a phone call from Harrison asking where his Moog was. Krause wrote, 'Feeling that I was speaking with a total idiot, I once again repeated the terms.' Beaver and Krause were just representatives for the Moog Corporation; they didn't have any control over the factory. They had already sold Moogs to George Martin and Mick Jagger, and it was clear from the urgency in his voice that George was feeling left out and couldn't understand why being a Beatle didn't entitle him to jump the queue. Eventually he understood and asked Krause to come over with the machine to clear it through customs and to show him how to use it. George said that he would pay all his expenses but nothing for his time. 'You're selling the bloody things. Now show me how to play it.' Bernie agreed. After one more phone call from George, a first-class ticket to London arrived in the mail. Krause immediately cashed it in, as you could in those days, for two economy seats so that his wife, Denise, could accompany him. He called Apple to make sure he was expected, which he was, and he and his wife left on a 707 for London.

They had been booked into the Dorchester, then, as now, one of the most expensive hotels in town. It turned out, however, that the day Bernie had called to confirm that everything was all right George had had his tonsils out and would not be able to see Bernie for a week. The Apple office had neglected to tell him. They said they would call him when George was ready to see him. As Krause had only allowed for one week in London to show George the ropes, he was understandably irritated. He decided to go on to Paris making sure that he left the number of his Paris hotel with George's assistant, several secretaries and the concierge of the Dorchester.

Every few days he called Apple to see if there was any news and each time was told that 'George will call when he's ready'. Then, after about a week, there came a furious call from London, 'Where the fuck have you been? George has been sitting around waiting for you for days!' It turned out that Apple was unable to get the synthesizer out of customs because no one there could define what it was and they were trying to tax it as an electronic device. Bernie told the caller, in no uncertain terms, where she could put her attitude and hung up. She soon called back, apologetic, and Bernie agreed to return to London in a couple of days. It was arranged that someone from Apple would meet him at Heathrow and take him straight to the customs section of the airport where the Moog was being held. Krause arranged for the driver to bring an amplifier with him. At customs he quickly unpacked the instrument, plugged in the amplifier, set the controls to make it sound like a Hammond B-3 organ and played the officer a couple of tunes. This did the trick. As an electronic device the customs duty would have been 60 or 70 per cent, a huge amount as the instrument cost $15,000; however, as an electronic organ the duty was less than 10 per cent. Bernie saved Apple a lot of money. The duty was paid, and the Moog III was allowed to enter the country.

Later that afternoon two cars arrived to take Bernie and Denise, separately, to George's house in Esher. Patti Boyd welcomed them and offered them food while George proffered a joint. George stressed that the food was vegetarian, as he stretched out on a large leather couch. George was the first of the Beatles to embrace vegetarianism, beginning as far back as 1965. Patti was possibly less keen. On a visit to Esher I remember George boasting how wonderful Patti's vegetarian food was and my wife, Sue, who was a cook, catching Patti's eye and them both nodding imperceptibly. They knew that the meal was so tasty because it contained chopped-up shrimps.

The Moog was set up against the wall across from the couch. In the corner was a multi-track and a two-track with tape cued up, ready to play. George said he wanted to play something to Bernie that he made on the synthesizer that he was planning to release on Zapple. He told him, 'It's my first electronic piece done with a little help from my cats.' In his autobiography, Krause recalls how at first he didn't recognize the material, then it slowly dawned upon him that the tape that George was playing was from the tape that he had made late at night after the Jackie Lomax sessions in Los Angeles a few months before. In fact George had only had a few hours alone with the Moog before Krause arrived, so it was clearly not made on George's own machine. Krause didn't know what to do, but eventually screwed up his courage and said, 'George, this is my music. Why is it on this tape, and why are you representing it as yours?' He reports that George assured him, 'Don't worry. I've edited it, and if it sells I'll send you a couple of quid.'

An argument quickly developed. Krause was understandably outraged to see his material appropriated and passed off as George's without being in any way consulted, and George was also getting angry that anyone would challenge his actions. Krause reported the exchange: '"You're coming on like you're Jimi Hendrix. When Ravi Shankar comes to my house, he's humble." Then . . . he screamed his most famous line, "Trust me, I'm a Beatle!"'[4]

Krause got up, and asked George to order him a car. There was no point in continuing the conversation. While they were waiting George asked him to set up a bagpipe sound, which Krause did without saying a word. Krause didn't have the money to sue George for plagiarism and probably didn't relish the thought of coming up against Apple's powerful lawyers either, so he just asked for his name to be taken off the acknowledgement on the cover. As we didn't expect the album to sell very well, it was decided that rather than reprint the sleeve we would just paint over Bernie's name – which was in any case spelled incorrectly as 'Crause' – with silver paint, which is what was done.

I had no role in any of this as I was in the USA the whole time that the record was in production. I was present only at one meeting, and that was the one in which the use of silver paint was decided. I didn't know the full story until years later, although there was a bit of muttering around Apple at the time. I was not keen on the record, as it was not the result of much experimentation or research, and hardly counted at all as a piece of electronic music; it was just George learning to use the Moog III synthesizer. Had it been by anyone else we would not have released it, but obviously the Beatles could do anything they wanted. Nor did I find John's and Yoko's album pleasurable in any sense, but it did have a kind of grim intensity and intelligence about it that I respected: they really did believe that everything they did was of such earth-shattering importance that it should be recorded for posterity and released. I was pleased to release it because I believed very much that throughout the course of the sixties rock 'n' roll had transformed itself from being a branch of the variety and entertainment business and had become an art form. The pop side still existed, but rock musicians were now telling the tale of the tribe, and the personal diary aspect of *Life with the Lions* fitted right into that.

'You're coming on like you're Jimi Hendrix. When Ravi Shankar comes to my house, he's humble.' Then . . . he screamed his most famous line, 'Trust me, I'm a Beatle!'

Chapter 15

Apple Crumble

John and Yoko with Allen Klein, who is pictured here representing Lennon
in negotiations over control of shares in the Beatles' Northern Songs company.
They orchestrated Klein's arrival at Apple, and Klein oversaw a wholesale change
of management that destroyed the original Apple team.

Apple Crumble

I HAD RETURNED FROM my recording trip to the USA to find a very different atmosphere at Apple. People were wary of each other and scared. This was because Allen Klein had been appointed first as an adviser, then as business manager of Apple. He had already been in to make lists of who did what. No one liked him, particularly Paul McCartney who remembered the way Klein had snared John:

> We were in some office. Klein was practising putting in one of those little things. You know, really suave in his dreadful brown pullover he used to wear, dreadful brown slacks and big pools of sweat underneath the arms, fucking hell, and his big sidies which he thought made him hip. He was just an 'orrible little man but with an amazing gift of the gab. 'Wadda ya want? Wadda ya want?' His dialogue would go, 'Wadda ya want?' 'Money.' 'Fantastic, you got it.' He said to John, 'Wadda ya want?' and John said, 'Yoko', and he said, 'You got it.'[1]

Klein quickly took on the role of the Brian Epstein/missing father figure for John and could do no wrong. He consolidated his position by firing as many people as he possibly could and installing his own people. It took a little while for him to figure out how far he could go, so he began with the small fry. Margo Stevens was an Apple Scruff, one of the fans who waited outside the door for a glimpse of their heroes, until Tony Bramwell hired her as the tea lady and she joined the kitchen staff. Klein fired her, so there was no tea. The cook was fired, so everyone went to restaurants. Then the translator was fired; this was foolish. Apple's records were released simultaneously in twenty-seven territories, meaning that sleeve printers and

record manufacturers, record company executives and press representatives in all those countries had to be contacted on the telephone and the entire operation coordinated in a dozen languages.
The translator usually did this, and without him there was chaos; it
was much less common to find English spoken outside Britain and
North America in those days.

The first major firing came on 8 May, when six executives and
their secretaries were sacked. Brian Lewis, in the contracts
department, went, and the publishing office was closed with all its
staff. One of the more obvious ones to go was 'Magic' Alex,
supposedly John Lennon's best friend, who returned from a trip to
Paris to find himself locked out of his workshop in Boston Place and
his contract terminated. He had applied for more than a hundred
patents, all of which had been refused on the grounds that they were
already patented ideas; as everyone suspected, Alex had a
subscription to *Popular Science*, and the Beatles didn't. The invisible
sonic screen never happened, the phone that called someone when
you spoke to it, the flying saucer, the wallpaper loudspeakers, were
all someone else's ideas or else pure fantasies. The 72-track recording
studio that he had been building in the basement of 3 Savile Row
was already well known to be a disaster: he hadn't realized that
studios have to be soundproofed, and you could hear people walking
on the floor above. Even worse was the building's central heating
unit which made a lot of noise and was also located in the basement.
It would have had to be turned off every time anyone wanted to
record. It was when George Harrison saw him preparing to install
seventy-two small speakers on the wall that they finally realized that
he knew less about recording studios than the tea lady. Long-
suffering George Martin was prevailed upon to come to the rescue;
he ripped out all of Alex's junk and installed machines borrowed
from EMI. Alex had not even known that the control room and the
studio had to be connected so that microphone leads and cables

could run between them, so for a short period cables ran down the corridor to connect the two. Alex's famous mixing deck was sold for £5 to a scrap electronics merchant on the Edgware Road.

It came as a complete shock when Alistair Taylor was fired. He had been with the Beatles from the Cavern days and was a close friend; it was Alistair whom they called up in the middle of the night to tell their problems to, or whom they paid visits to unexpectedly after midnight to get drunk with or cry on his shoulder, whom they turned to for comfort over losing their girlfriends. He was one of the Liverpool group of totally loyal staff who adored the boys and were there out of love, not for the money. Alistair never took kickbacks – although accused of it by Linda McCartney (née Eastman) – and was, like Neil Aspinall, Mal Evans and Peter Brown, more of a royal courtier than a record business employee. It turned out that their loyalty was misplaced. Rather than let Klein fire him, Peter Brown told him the news. Alistair choked back tears and spent the rest of the day trying to reach Paul and John on the phone, but they wouldn't take his calls.

That same day saw Ron Kass dismissed. Klein had been gunning for him since he arrived and finally got him by alleging financial impropriety. It was a false accusation, but he managed to sow the seeds of doubt in the four Beatles' minds (the full story is in Peter Brown's book, *The Love You Make*). Kass had done an exemplary job in running Apple Records, given how difficult the Beatles had made it for him, and the sacking was utterly unwarranted. Fortunately he had a good contract; I thought he should sue Klein for slander, but Ron said he had been expecting it. That same day Peter Brown, in his position as an Apple director, signed over the lease of the town house in Mayfair that Kass was living in. Brown wrote, 'I got supreme pleasure in seeing Kass get that town house.' Ron was replaced by Jack Oliver, who had previously been Terry Doran's personal assistant. He knew nothing about running a record company, which is why Klein put him in that position.

Things were made so unbearable that Denis O'Dell, head of the film department, who had been producing Ringo in *The Magic Christian*, resigned. He had sensibly kept his office at Twickenham Film Studios and no doubt also had a good contract. I met him a few times, and it was obvious that he wouldn't have remained at Apple very long; he was too professional and had been in the business since 1951 and could see disaster coming.

In June, shortly after Kass was fired, Peter Asher resigned. He told *Disc and Music Echo*:

> When I joined Apple the idea was that it would be different from the other companies in the record business. Its policy was to help people and be generous. It didn't mean actually I had a tremendous amount of freedom; I was always in danger of one Beatle saying, 'Yes, that's a great idea, go ahead', and then another coming in and saying he didn't know anything about it. But it did mean that it was a nice company to work for. Now that's all changed.

Klein installed his number-one man from the New York office, Peter Howard, as financial director. From now on Apple was a straight business, employees had to sign in and out with time cards and it became a thoroughly unpleasant place to work if you were on the staff. John and Yoko installed themselves in Ron Kass's former office and were there virtually every day, giving interviews, promoting their various films and projects. This was another cause of resentment in the building: Yoko used to bring her daughter Kyoko into the office, and she was allowed to run and play as she pleased. She took to pulling the plugs out of Laurie's telephone switchboard, cutting off transatlantic calls and major business discussions, but no one was allowed to intervene. Then John Lennon got cut off mid-call. But instead of stopping her he yelled at Laurie as if it had been

'Z' is for Zapple.

Introducing Zapple, a new label from Apple Records.

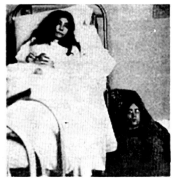

John Lennon/Yoko Ono: 'Life with the Lions:
(Zapple 01) Unfinished Music No.2.'

George Harrison: 'Electronic Sound.'
(Zapple 02)

Amid the disintegration of Apple and despite the spectre of Zapple's
demise, *Life with the Lions* and *Electronic Sound* were released and
promoted as Zapple records, as shown by this advertisement in *OZ*

her fault. They had fired the kitchen staff as a money-saving operation, but Yoko had a £15 tin of caviar delivered every day from nearby Fortnum and Mason's, usually leaving the unfinished tin out to spoil instead of putting it in the fridge, so that the next day she began another one. The chef's wages had been £12 a week. The other Beatles stayed away, and Apple became John's and Yoko's office.

I was concerned because it seemed inevitable that the Zapple label would be axed even though it had only just been launched, on 1 May in the USA and 9 May in the UK. Klein couldn't fire me because I wasn't on the staff; nevertheless, I felt considerable sympathy for my friends there and was dismayed when Peter Asher said he was leaving. I also felt a certain loyalty to those artists I had recorded – Olson, Weaver, Ferlinghetti, McClure, Bukowski and Brautigan – and wanted their records to be released. I had also spent a lot of time preparing for Allen Ginsberg's album. Peter advised me to stay on and do whatever I could. He said to go to New York and record the Ginsberg album and intimated that Ron Kass, who had gone straight on to become the new head of MGM Records in Hollywood, might well release it if Zapple didn't. Emboldened, I flew to New York to begin work with Allen.

When I joined Apple the idea was
that it would be different from
the other companies in the record
business. Its policy was to help
people and be generous.

Chapter 16

The Second Trip: Allen Ginsberg

The Second Trip: Allen Ginsberg

K EN WEAVER HAD MOVED to Tucson, Arizona, so I needed a hotel. Allen suggested that I stay at the Hotel Chelsea on West 23rd Street, 'This is where you belong,' he said. He was right. I finished up living there for a number of years. He insisted on inspecting the room, number 420, to make sure it wasn't too ratty. The first thing to do before we began recording was to arrange Allen's contract. The contracts for the albums I had already recorded had been done by Apple's contract department. This one would have to be written by Allen Klein. Allen and I went to see him at 1700 Broadway. Iris Keitel showed us in.

Klein's office had tall double doors made from heavy beaten copper, which looked like something Klein had picked up from the auction of the *Cleopatra* set in Hollywood. It was a power office, with two sides of glass, looking out over Central Park and the surrounding skyscrapers of mid-Manhattan. Klein sat slumped behind an empty desk which seemed much too big for him, with his hands on the desk. He didn't get up. He wore a dirty white T-shirt; it looked as if he'd been reading the *New York Times* where the ink always comes off on your fingers and finds its way on to your clothes. Although Klein was very used to meeting famous people in showbusiness, he seemed genuinely interested to meet Allen who came from a different world. He wanted to discuss Allen's political opinions, the Vietnam War and Allen's philosophy. I don't think it was a strategy but a genuine interest; however, we soon got down to business. He had proposed a contract that gave Apple all the rights and none to Allen.

Allen's early background was in advertising, and his brother Eugene was a lawyer and had had a look at the contract. A side of

Allen emerged that I had not previously seen, that of the canny businessman. Allen suggested that the basis of a contract was that two people agree to do something together, and the contract formalizes this intention, whereas he saw Klein's attitude as essentially confrontational. They talked about this for a while but when Klein wouldn't move Allen insisted on his rights. 'Assuming I trust you,' he said, 'how do I know you're always going to be here as head of Apple? You might go down into Central Park one afternoon and rape a little girl on her way home from school.' He pointed out of the window up Broadway towards the park. 'Then you'd go to gaol and I'd have to deal with a stranger who didn't understand the nature of our deal.' This visibly shocked Klein, who span around in his huge leather office chair, 'That's absurd!' he shouted. 'I have a wife and children. I wouldn't do a thing like that. You're just saying that to try and shock me, to be obscene!' But he wouldn't let it go; Allen was famous for his words, and Klein wanted to talk. He discussed pornography and censorship, and in the end the meeting lasted more than an hour, with only one short break when Klein shouted at someone in Australia. Klein seemed to like Allen, or more accurately he seemed fascinated by him, but we emerged from his office with no deal in place. Klein said he would prepare another outline contract but in the meantime we should go ahead and start recording. We were to use Capitol Records' midtown studio on Broadway, wholly owned by EMI in London, which had a deal with Apple.

I discussed the album with Allen in great detail, and we decided that each track should be treated individually, with its own selected instrumentation, rather than assemble a group of sympathetic musicians and have them back Allen on every track like a band. Thus some tracks were virtually solo and others had a number of instruments. One time we went for a more Elizabethan-sounding arrangement, and another we opted for a country-and-western feel.

TELEPHONE MESSAGE

BRESLAW PRINTING CO., N.Y.
STOCK FORM NO. 715

PRINTED IN U.S.A.

7/19/69 19 ___ Time 12 ³¹ M.

M _____
Room 604

THE FOLLOWING MESSAGE WAS RECEIVED
DURING YOUR ABSENCE, FROM

M _____ Tel. No. _____

Mr Alan
Ginsberg
Music Shertrone finished
Call me (New #)
607 264-6811

TELEPHONE MESSAGE

BRESLAW PRINTING CO., N.Y.
STOCK FORM NO. 715

PRINTED IN U.S.A.

_____ 19 ___ Time 1 ⁰⁵ p M.

M _____
Room 604

THE FOLLOWING MESSAGE WAS RECEIVED
DURING YOUR ABSENCE, FROM

M ___ Call ___ Tel. No. _____

Michael Hollingshead
448 3858

The Hotel Chelsea has housed many notable writers and artists over the years, including William Burroughs, Dylan Thomas, Bob Dylan, Arthur C. Clarke, Janis Joplin, Leonard Cohen, the Grateful Dead, Larry Rivers and Mark Rothko . . . to name just a few.

Above: Expenses receipts and ephemera from the Hotel Chelsea, which became the author Barry Miles's home away from home.

But first we had to find the musicians and an arranger. Fortunately Allen knew the perfect arranger: Bob Dorough, cool jazz pianist, composer, songwriter, all-round bebop-era jazzman and one of the few performers to sing a vocal on a Miles Davis record.[1] With his experience as a producer and arranger he was the perfect man for the job – better suited than me in fact, but he never pulled rank and was a pleasure to work with. Next we had to find musicians. Bob Dorough was a fine keyboard player, and I thought that for most tracks we would also need a guitarist and a bass player, and, beyond that, it would depend upon the arrangements.

Allen immediately suggested we go to see Charles Mingus and ask if he would play on the album. This was beyond my wildest dreams. We went to the Village Vanguard where Mingus was playing[2] and after his set we went backstage. He was friendly but seemed a little spaced out. This was his empty period; he had not released a record since January 1966. He said to come to visit him and bring a tape of the material we had. The next afternoon, on a blazing hot day, Allen and I walked over to Avenue C and down to East 5th Street. Mingus lived at the end of the dead-end block going west. The street was filled with overflowing garbage bins, and the burnt-out shell of a car, robbed of everything that could be sold, stood outside his building. I think we woke him up, even though it was about 3 p.m., because he seemed woozy. He wore just a pair of sagging underpants, and sweat ran like river tributaries down his round stomach. He found us orange juice from the fridge.

It was a railroad apartment, and the first room was filled with old newspapers and mysterious plastic bags, stacked high with a corridor between. In his living-room he gestured to the tape-recorder, and I threaded on Allen's demo tape. I had a pick-up reel with me in case there were none available. Allen had written a number of songs since the tape was made and these he sang, accompanying himself on his Indian harmonium. Mingus hushed

Allen and listened closely to the tape and to Allen's recital. Then he gave a careful analysis of Allen's music. His voice was terrible and would need strengthening, Peter should be left out completely, the tracks were raw and should stay that way, Allen's timing was off but could be fixed by a good walking bass. He said it was good work but he didn't think he could play on it; it wasn't jazz. We asked if he could recommend a good bass player and he said that Herman Wright was our man if he would do it. Well, that would be great, I thought. I knew his work with the Chet Baker Quintet and with Yusef Lateef, and it would be an honour to work with someone so accomplished. (I had never expected Mingus to actually play with Allen.) Charles gave us the details, and we had a meeting with Herman and he immediately understood what we were trying to do and agreed to play on it. He finished up on six of the twenty-one tracks.

While Bob worked on the arrangements we looked for musicians and rehearsed the material. The photographer Robert Frank, an old friend of Ginsberg (and Kerouac and the Beats), let us use the huge front room of his apartment on West Side Drive on the Upper West Side. I thought we would start with the simplest pieces to get Allen used to the microphone and for him to learn microphone technique. 'The Human Abstract' was just Allen singing with his Indian harmonium, and there were several others that at this point had no instrumentation other than guitar.

I had thought that EMI Abbey Road was old-fashioned, but at Capitol the recording engineers not only wore white lab coats but had little leather holsters in which they kept their tape-editing scissors. They were so experienced and skilful that they disdained a tape-editing block – a metal block with a 45-degree groove cut into it – and simply held the tape in one hand and made a perfect 45-degree cut across it. Then they did the same to the tape they were editing and applied the splicing tape. I was impressed. I was less impressed by their openly disdainful attitude toward Allen and Peter Orlovsky. These were old-style big-band variety showbiz people, and the countercultural music of the late sixties had not yet penetrated their consciousness. However, we were paying, and they did what we asked them. The trouble was that Mingus was right; Peter's voice was so bad there was little we could do with it. He was still taking amphetamines, and he still had his 'leper's voice'. It was loud, flat and out of tune, with no redeeming qualities. We mixed it down as low as possible before Allen objected. We did two or three sessions and had two tracks done when the inevitable and expected happened. Allen Klein closed Zapple without informing me or anyone in the Apple office. Capitol would accept no more studio bookings and refused to hand over the existing tapes unless I paid for them; they clearly didn't trust Klein's office to pay. I was stuck with studio bills and a hotel bill at the Chelsea. I tried Paul McCartney at home but was always told he was out, and none of the Beatles could be reached at Apple. Eventually, after a few days of worry, Derek Taylor got authorization – I think from George Harrison – to pay off my debts (but not the studio bills) and I was able to rest easy again. Meanwhile, with so much preparation and work already done, Allen decided that he would pay for the recording himself and we would lease it to a record company. I estimated that the studio costs and the musicians would amount to about $10,000, and Allen felt he could manage that. I called Peter Asher to discuss the idea of releasing it on MGM. Ron Kass had moved from running Apple Records to become the head of MGM Records and had hired Peter as his head of A&R. It was the old team back together again. 'Come and discuss it,' Peter said.

Mingus lived at the end of the dead-
end block going west. The street
was filled with overflowing garbage
bins, and the burnt-out shell of a
car, robbed of everything that could
be sold, stood outside his building . . .
He wore just a pair of sagging
underpants, and sweat ran like river
tributaries down his round stomach.

Chapter 17

The Second Trip: LA

The Second Trip: LA

I FLEW FROM NEW York to Los Angeles and headed straight for TT&G Studios where Frank Zappa was recording. He had offered to put me up and suggested that I meet him there, catch some of the sessions and then go back with him to Woodrow Wilson Drive where he lived. TT&G stood for 'Two Terrible Guys' – Ami Hadani and Tom Hidley. It was at 1441 North McCadden Place near the intersection of Sunset and Highland in Hollywood. It was where parts of *The Velvet Underground and Nico*, the Velvet Underground's first album, had been recorded and was designed for modern rock music, with high decibel levels. Frank was recording *Hot Rats* when I arrived. Captain Beefheart was there, and Johnny Otis, the legendary bandleader, was the session leader. I was suddenly back in the heart of the rock-'n'-roll business. Frank was very interested to hear all the gossip about Klein and the break-up of Apple. I told him that I was doing an album with Allen Ginsberg, and he recommended that we use Apostolic Studios in New York, where he had made *We're Only in It for the Money*, *Lumpy Gravy*, *Uncle Meat* and *Cruisin' With Ruben and the Jets*.

The purpose of the trip was of course to firm up the deal with MGM, but there were no problems there; they were happy to lease the album, and I met the art department personnel and the other people I would be dealing with as producer. Ron Kass, Peter Asher and I stood in Ron's palatial office, with its Picasso prints, and looked out over a livid orange-and-red Los Angeles sunset, touched glasses and laughed. It did seem a whole lot better than the bickering and backbiting at Savile Row. The visit to MGM is one of those examples of a road not travelled. It seemed that there was work at MGM if I wanted it, going through all the back catalogue – people like Sham the Sham – and planning a reissue series; also reissues of the Velvet Underground and of course the Mothers of Invention's early records, which were all on MGM-Verve. As I knew Zappa, and was in fact staying with him and he seemed to trust me, I was sure we could have worked together. There was also the possibility of getting together with Valerie. It was all food for thought.

Back in New York we were ready to begin rehearsals. Bob had finished his arrangements, and we now had our musicians: Janet Zeitz on flute, Cyril Caster on guitar, trumpet and French horn, Jon Sholle, a multi-instrumentalist who played autoharp, electric bass, guitar and drums on the album, and of course Herman Wright on stand-up bass. Bob Dorough played piano and organ on many of the tracks. I made a block booking at Apostolic Studios, and we began.

Apostolic was downtown, at 53 East 10th Street – it was very rare in those days to find recording studios outside the midtown music business because everyone said that no one would go downtown to record. It was $95 an hour and $115 an hour after midnight.

It was named after their prototype twelve-track Scully tape-recorder: a huge machine about six feet long that Paul Berkowitz, the maintenance engineer, stripped down every weekend. There was an in-house astrologer who each day cast the i-ching or studied his coffee grounds or something and who sometimes decided that the signs were so bad that no recording should be done that day. Fortunately the signs were propitious throughout the six weeks or so we were there. The studio engineer and tape operator was Dave Baker, who had a laid-back, easy, friendly manner and to our amazement was a Coca-Cola afficionado who could identify which bottling plant a bottle of Coca-Cola came from. Unlike Capitol, these people appreciated working with Ginsberg. I was most impressed with the technical know-how and the equipment: it was the world's first twelve-track (although sixteen-track rapidly overtook it). It was a funky studio, with clippings from newspapers and photographs pinned on the wall. In the control booth was an illustration from a fifties trade magazine entitled 'How to hold a large rabbit' showing a serious-looking farmer supporting a rabbit the size of an eight-year-old child. This was also the first place I saw a mock-German warning to inquisitive visitors, although it had apparently been around since the early fifties:

ACHTUNG! ALLES LOOKENSPEEPERS!
Das computermachine ist nicht fuer gefingerpoken und mitten grabben.
Ist easy schnappen der springen werk, blowenfusen und poppencorken mit spitzensparken.
Ist nicht fuer gewerken bei das dumpkopfen.
Das rubbernecken sichtseeren keepen das cotten-pickenen hans in das pockets muss; relaxen und watchen das blinkenlichten.

Allen's time-keeping was unconventional and changed from line to line according to the meaning of the text. A traditional rhythm section was therefore out of the question, which is why there were no drums on most of the tracks. The time-keeping duties fell to the keyboards or bass who could drop in or out whenever needed but could also be used to strengthen Allen's voice. Much of the charm of Allen's renditions of Blake's songs came from his untrained, somewhat uncertain singing, although I hoped we could correct some of the more out-of-tune notes with overdubs and double track-ing. A number of other devices were used to strengthen his voice: a bass following the vocal line instead of keeping time, an organ swell to distract from a flat note, a trill or sweetener to balance a certain

This page and opposite: Miles, Ginsberg and the team work on the recording of Ginsberg's rendition of *Songs of Innocence and of Experience* by William Blake.

Top left: Bob Dorough, Miles, Allen Ginsberg and Janet Zeitz.

dryness. This was Allen's first musical outing on record, and I still feel that the songs get closer to how Blake would have sung them in Soho pubs and friends' houses than any of the 'serious' classical musical settings of them.

Herman Wright made a major contribution to the recordings. On 'The Echoing Green' he compensated for the weakness in Allen's voice by playing the vocal line in a lower register when Allen sang high notes and emphasized the depth of voice and feeling at the end of the song. His plucked bass and Bob Dorough's piano were used to keep the tune jolly before its slightly sinister ending.

Allen always sang 'The Lamb' as a duet with Peter Orlovsky, so to make Peter's amphetamine vocals more acceptable we aimed for a medieval street-fair sound with Janet Zeitz on flute, Bob Dorough on organ and Cyril Caster on guitar. I sat Allen and Peter cross-legged on the studio floor to keep them in microphone range. Don Cherry joined the sessions and played various forms of percussion on five of the tracks. Everyone played on 'The Laughing Song': Cyril Caster on trumpet and French horn, Janet Zeitz on flute and amplified flute; Bob Dorough kept the beat steady with the harpsichord, with Don Cherry providing percussion. Everyone in the studio joined in the chorus including Michael Aldrich, the editor of *Marijuana Review*, and Matt Hoffman, the studio manager. The ending was put on a tape loop and then faded into infinity. Allen's vocalizing on 'The Garden of Love' suggested a country-and-western treatment, since that was how he was already phrasing it on the demo tapes. The guitar, bass and drums were all overdubbed by John Sholle. This track inspired the poet and Fug vocalist Ed Sanders, who was at the session, to record several country-and-western albums at Apostolic including the memorable *Beercans on the Moon*.

The most exciting track to work on for me was 'The Grey Monk' because Allen managed to get Elvin Jones to play on it. Jones was in the John Coltrane Quartet and played on many of my favourite albums including *My Favorite Things, Africa Brass* and *A Love Supreme*, so it was an honour to meet him. His tiny Japanese wife Keiko came in first, carrying a huge drum kit, followed by Elvin in shades. She produced a hammer and nails and fixed the kit to the studio floor. The staff were somewhat aghast but said nothing. After one run-through we recorded the track in just two takes. Both times Elvin was perfect, ending the track with a terrific drum roll. He collected his $500 and left. (Years later he and Allen taught together in a progressive school in Florida.)

We wanted the album to reach the youth market, not just literary types, so I commissioned Michael McInnerney to design the sleeve. Mike was an old friend of mine and had recently done the sleeve for *Tommy* by the Who. Back in Britain I went up to Cambridge and spent a day in the Fitzwilliam Museum, selecting William Blake images to use on the cover. I narrowed it down to six of his coloured illustrations to his *Songs of Innocence and of Experience*, and, after Allen's approval, Mike began work. The album was issued as a gate-fold, with an extra page tipped in to enable Allen to write a lengthy text about Blake, the poems and his interpretation of them. This was the first album suggested for Zapple and the last to be recorded. Without the Beatles it would never have happened because they provided the initial impetus, but thanks to Peter Asher and Ron Kass it did finally get made.

One event that did not seem significant at the time, but which later became known as an important turning point in our culture, came on 28 June. We had just finished recording for the day. It was about 4 a.m., and Allen suggested that we walk along to the Stonewall Bar, on Christopher Street, to see what was happening. The previous night there had been a riot there. The anti-homosexual law in New York specified that men were not allowed to dance with each other, which naturally gave the police the chance to raid homosexual clubs and often meant that gay clubs and bars were making heavy payments to the police to stay open. In the hot, humid weather of late June in New York some routine police harassment at the Stonewall Bar had resulted in, instead of the usual passivity and intimidation, the gays swarming out of the club and smashing the police-car window.

Allen and I arrived to find the club still open but a line of police barricades surrounding it. There had been another riot earlier that night, with about a thousand people there, some with banners, blocking the street and many police cars, their red lights revolving. Allen approached the police line, with me in tow, and the first cop he reached asked for his autograph. The actual riot was over, but there was still sporadic shouting of insults and a tense atmosphere. This friendly act seemed to calm things down. Allen shook his hand, and after a lot of conversation with various members of the crowd joining in we went into the club. There were only about half a dozen people there; most were outside. I had a beer at the bar while Allen danced with one of the regulars. 'Like a galleon in full sail', as Allen later described himself to me. Scuffles and the occasional shouting match continued for several more nights, but essentially the victory was with the gay community and the law was repealed. The Stonewall Riots marked the beginning of a movement for gay recognition that continues today.

Allen's album received respectful reviews, including a good one from *Rolling Stone*. The *Blake Newsletter* liked it, saying that it sounded more authentic than the high-art classical settings of Blake's songs. As this book was being written, a mention appeared online suggesting that the album has not been completely forgotten:

When we think of sixties-defining albums, we think of *Blonde on Blonde*, *Are You Experienced?*, *Sgt Pepper's Lonely Hearts Club Band*, that sort of thing, and rightly so, but a project like *Songs*

SONGS OF INNOCENCE AND EXPERIENCE
by William Blake, tuned by Allen Ginsberg

The cover art from the album *Songs of Innocence and Experience by William Blake, tuned by Allen Ginsberg.*

Album details include the following:

Arrangements by Allen Ginsberg, Bob Dorough, Cyril Caster,
Lee Crabtree and Jonathan Sholle

Produced by Miles Associates for Allen Ginsberg and Peter Orlovsky

Engineer: Dave Baker

Recorded at Apostolic Studios, New York City, June and July 1969

Artwork: Front cover background by Michael McInnerney, illustrations
by William Blake. The Blake reproductions are by kind permission of the
Trustees of the Fitzwilliam Museum. Cambridge, England.

Music © May King Poetry Music

A new edition of the album will be released by Ginsberg Recordings
on Record Store Day, 16 April 2016.

of Innocence and Experience by William Blake, Tuned by Allen Ginsberg speaks just as much to what became possible in that artistic Cambrian explosion of an era.[1]

Ron Kass, Peter Asher and I stood
in Ron's palatial office, with its
Picasso prints, and looked out over
a livid orange-and-red Los Angeles
sunset, touched glasses and laughed.
It did seem a whole lot better than
the bickering and backbiting at
Savile Row.

Chapter 18

Meanwhile Back in the USA

'And in the end . . .' George Harrison, John Lennon, Paul McCartney and Ringo Starr,
9 April 1969. The autographs above were signed on the flyleaf of a 1968 copy
of Hunter Davis's *The Beatles*. Apple Scruff Carol Bedford got all four Beatles to
sign the book in person. George Harrison signed it at his home for her at Easter 1969.
John Lennon, Paul McCartney and Ringo Starr signed it on the steps of the
EMI Studios on Abbey Road while the group was recording the *Abbey Road* album
in the summer of 1969. Courtesy of the Mark Naboshek Collection.

Meanwhile Back in the USA

I DID MAKE ONE final trip that year. First to New York, back to the Hotel Chelsea, then to Los Angeles, to deliver the album sleeve artwork to Peter Asher at MGM. Valerie came to stay with me at Frank Zappa's house.

I regretted the fact that Zapple didn't work out. The Beatles regretted the fact that Apple didn't work out. John Lennon told me:

John: Apple was a manifestation of Beatle naïvety, collective naïvety, and we said we're going to do this and help everybody and all that. And we got conned just on the subtlest and the most grossest level. We didn't really get approached by the best artists, or any of the recording thing, we got all the bums from everywhere – they'd been thrown out from everywhere else. And the other people who were really groovy wouldn't approach us because they're too proud.

Miles: Or maybe they don't like hustling.

John: They don't like hustling, of course. I couldn't hustle.

Miles: But the only way to reach you people is to hustle.

John: Right, and that's why it didn't work. And then we have to quickly build up another wall round us to protect us from all the beggars and lepers in Britain and America that came up to us, and the vibes are getting insane. And I tried, when we were at Wigmore Street, to see everyone, like we said, 'You don't have to get down on your knees' – I saw everyone day in day out and there wasn't anybody with anything to offer to society or me or anything. There was just 'I want, I want' and why not? Terrible scenes going on in the office with different spades and hippies and all different people getting very wild with me. Even the peace campaign – we had a lot of that too, but once you've opened the door it's hard, you know. That's all it is. It's just different.[1]

It was worse for them. They had a staff and buildings and companies to deal with, and it took years to wind down. As far as John, George and Ringo were concerned, it also cost them millions of pounds to extricate themselves from the lupine grip of Klein – Paul had wisely refused to sign a management contract with him. Klein finally got his dues: in 1979 he went to gaol for two months for tax evasion after stealing the proceeds from the sale of promotional copies of the *Concert for Bangladesh* charity album and delaying the release of funds from the concert for years.

I personally felt a great responsibility towards all the people I had recorded and also, naturally, wanted to see my work released. I found ways to release most of their albums, the first being *Listening to Richard Brautigan* which came out on EMI-Harvest in 1970, which was the label that would have distributed Zapple in the USA had it survived. I met with Moe Ashe, and he agreed to release Charles Olson's *Maximus IV, V, VI* on Folkways; it appeared two years later. Ferlinghetti's tapes appeared on a number of different Fantasy albums, but unfortunately the original album, as envisaged, never came into being. The Bukowski tapes were not released until 1998, by which time albums had been replaced by CDs. *At Terror Street and Agony Way* came out as a double disc from King Mob. The Ken Weaver and Michael McClure tapes were never finished and were not properly edited. The dream was over.

How to end the story? This is the last press release issued by Derek Taylor, typed by Mavis Smith, after Klein closed down the Apple press office and gave the job to an agency:

10 April 1970

Spring is here and Leeds play Chelsea tomorrow, and Ringo and John and George and Paul are alive and well and full of hope.

The world is still spinning and so are we and so are you.

When the spinning stops – that'll be the time to worry. Not before.

Until then, the Beatles are alive and well, and the Beat goes on, the Beat goes on.

BEAT
S ON

The Artists

Bibliography of works by the poets and writers recorded for Zapple up until February 1969:

Richard Brautigan

The Return of the Rivers, San Francisco, Inferno Press, 1957 (free distribution)

The Galilee Hitch-Hiker, San Francisco, White Rabbit Press, 1958

Lay the Marble Tea, San Francisco, Carp Press, 1959

The Octopus Frontier, San Francisco, Carp Press, 1960

All Watched Over By Machines of Loving Grace, San Francisco, Communication
  Company, 1967 (free distribution)

Please Plant This Book, San Francisco, self-published, 1968 (eight seed packets in
  folder, each with a poem printed on it) (free distribution)

The Pill Versus the Springhill Mine Disaster, San Francisco, Four Seasons
  Foundation, 1968

A Confederate General from Big Sur, New York, Grove Press, 1964

Trout Fishing in America, San Francisco, Four Seasons Foundation, 1967

In Watermelon Sugar, San Francisco, Four Seasons Foundation, 1968

Charles Bukowski

Flower, Fist and Bestial Wall, Eureka, CA, Hearse Press, 1959

Longshot Pomes for Broke Players, New York, 7 Poets Press, 1962

Run with the Hunted, Chicago, Midwest Poetry Chapbooks, 1962

Poems and Drawings, Crescent City, FL, Epos, a *Quarterly of Poetry*, 1962
  (entire issue)

It Catches My Heart in Its Hand, New Orleans, Loujon Press, 1963

Grip the Walls, Storrs, CT, *Wormwood Review* 16, 1964 (special eight-page section
  bound in)

Crucifix in a Deathhand, New Orleans, Loujon Press, 1965

Cold Dogs in the Courtyard, Chicago, Literary Times-Cyfoeth, 1965

Confessions of a Man Insane Enough to Live with Beasts, Bensonville, IL,

    Open Skull Press, 1965

All the Assholes in the World and Mine, Bensonville, IL, Open Skull Press, 1966

True Story, Santa Rosa, CA, Black Sparrow Press, 1966

On Going Out to Get the Mail, Santa Rosa, CA, Black Sparrow Press, 1966

To Kiss the Worms Goodnight, Santa Rosa, CA, Black Sparrow Press, 1966

The Girls, Santa Rosa, CA, Black Sparrow Press, 1966

The Flower Lover, Santa Rosa, CA, Black Sparrow Press, 1966

Night's Work, Stockton, CA, Wormwood Review Press, 1966

2 by Bukowski, Santa Rosa, CA, Black Sparrow Press, 1967

The Curtains Are Waving, Santa Rosa, CA, Black Sparrow Press, 1967

At Terror Street and Agony Way, Santa Rosa, CA, Black Sparrow Press, 1968

Poems Written Before Jumping Out of an 8-Story Window, Salt Lake City, UT,

    Litmus, Poetry X/Change, 1968

Notes of a Dirty Old Man, North Hollywood, CA, Essex House, 1969

Lawrence Ferlinghetti

Pictures of the Gone World, San Francisco, City Lights, 1955

A Coney Island of the Mind, New York, New Directions, 1958

Tentative Description of a Dinner Given to Promote the Impeachment of President

    Eisenhower, San Francisco, Golden Mountain Press, 1958 (broadside)

Her, New York, New Directions, 1960

Berlin, San Francisco, Golden Mountain Press, 1961 (broadside)

One Thousand Fearful Words for Fidel Castro, San Francisco, City Lights, 1961 (broadside)

Starting from San Francisco, New York, New Directions, 1961

Unfair Arguments with Existence, New York, New Directions, 1963 (short plays)

Thoughts of a Concerto of Telemann, San Francisco, Four Seasons Foundation, 1963

Where is Vietnam? San Francisco, Golden Mountain Press, 1963 (broadside);

    City Lights Books, 1965

Routines, New York, New Directions, 1964 (plays)

To Fuck Is to Love Again (Kyrie Eleison Kerista); or, The Situation in the West,

    Followed by a Holy Proposal, New York, Fuck You Press, 1965

Christ Climbed Down, Syracuse, NY, Syracuse University Press, 1965

Two Scavengers in a Truck, Two Beautiful People in a Mercedes, San Francisco,
    City Lights, 1968

An Eye on the World: Selected Poems, London, MacGibbon and Kee, 1967

Moscow in the Wilderness, Segovia in the Snow, San Francisco, Beach Books, 1967

After the Cries of the Birds, San Francisco, Dave Haselwood Books, 1967

Fuclock, London, Fire Publications, 1968

Reverie Smoking Grass, Milano, East 128, 1968

The Secret Meaning of Things, New York, New Directions, 1969

Tyrannus Nix?, New York, New Directions, 1969

Allen Ginsberg

Howl for Carl Solomon, San Francisco, self-published, 1956

Siesta in Xbalba, Near Icy Cape, Alaska, self-published, 1956

Howl and Other Poems, San Francisco, City Lights Books, 1956

Kaddish and Other Poems, San Francisco, City Lights Books, 1961

Empty Mirror, New York, Totem Press, 1961

Reality Sandwiches, San Francisco, City Lights Books, 1963

The Change, London, Writers' Forum, 1963

Wichita Vortex Sutra, London, Peace News, 1966

Prose Contribution to Cuban Revolution, Detroit, Artists' Workshop Press, 1966

T. V. Baby Poems, London, Cape Goliard Press, 1967

Scrap Leaves, New York, Poets' Press, 1968

Airplane Dreams, Toronto, Anansi, 1968

Wales: A Visitation, London, Cape Goliard Press, 1968

Ankor Wat, London, Fulcrum Press, 1968

Planet News, San Francisco, City Lights Books, 1968

Song and Sunflower Sutra, Milano, Fernanda Pivano, 1969

Michael McClure

Passage, Big Sur, CA, Jonathan Williams, 1956

Peyote Poem, San Francisco, Wallace Berman, 1958 (broadside included in *Semina* 3)

For Artaud, New York, Totem Press, 1959

Hymns to St Geryon and Other Poems, San Francisco, Auerhahn Press, 1959

We're in the Middle of a Deep Cloud, San Francisco, Wallace Berman, 1959
    (broadside included in *Semina* 4)

OH CHRIST GOD LOVE CRY OF LOVE STIFFLED FURRED, San Francisco,
    Auerhahn Press, 1959 (broadside included in *The Auerhahn Press*)

FUCK DEATH, San Francisco, privately published, 1959 (folded card)

! THE FEAST !, San Francisco, The Batman Gallery, 1960 (mimeographed sheets)

WE ARE IMPERVIOUS AS THE SKIN OF OUR DREAMS, Los Angeles,
    Wallace Berman, 1960 (broadside included in *Semina* 5)

The New Book / A Book of Torture, New York, Grove Press, 1961

Pillow, New York, New York Poets Theatre, 1961 (photocopied sheets)

Spontaneous Hymn to Kundalini, New Orleans, Loujon Press, 1961 (broadside)

Dark Brown, San Francisco, Auerhahn Press, 1961

Meat Science Essays, San Francisco, City Lights Books, 1963; City Lights,
    expanded edition 1966

GRAHHR GROOOOOOOOOOOOO NYARR GARHOOOOOOOSH ROSE,
    San Francisco, privately published, 1963 (broadside, containing only one line)

Love Lion Lioness, San Francisco, privately published, 1964 (poster)

DOUBLE MURDER! VAHROOOOOOOR!, Los Angeles, Wallace Berman, 1964
    (broadside included in *Semina* 9)

Poetry Is a Muscular Principle, Los Angeles, privately published, 1964 (broadside)

BLUE-BLACK WINGED SPACE RAINBOW, San Francisco, privately published,
    1964 (broadside, containing only one line)

Two For Bruce Conner, San Francisco, Oyez, 1964 (broadside)

13 Mad Sonnets, Milano, East 128, 1964

Ghost Tantras, San Francisco, privately published, 1964

Dream Table, San Francisco, Dave Haselwood, 1965 (set of thirty cards)

The Beard, San Francisco, privately published, 1965

Poisoned Wheat, San Francisco, privately published, 1965; Coyote 1966

Unto Caesar, San Francisco, Dave Haselwood, 1965

[Mandalas] with *Bruce Conner*, San Francisco, Dave Haselwood, 1966

(title is a mandala)

LOBE KEY STILLED LIONMAN LACED WINGED APRIL RAPHAEL

DANCE WIRY, with *Bruce Conner*, San Francisco, Dave Haselwood, 1966

(an envelope containing twenty-six cards)

Love Lion Book, San Francisco, Four Seasons Foundation, 1966

The Beard, San Francisco, Coyote, 1967; Grove Press, 1967

WAR IS DECOR IN MY CAVERN CAVE, San Francisco, Communication

Company, 1967 (broadside)

The Blossom, or Billy the Kid, Milwaukee, Great Lakes Books, 1967

Freewheelin' Frank, Secretary of the Angels, by Frank Reynolds, as Told to Michael

McClure, New York, Grove Press, 1967

#189, Oakland, Egg Press, 1967 (broadside)

*HAIL THEE WHO PLAY, Los Angeles, Black Sparrow Press, 1968

Little Odes: Jan–March 1961, New York, Poets' Press, 1968

The Sermons of Jean Harlow and the Curses of Billy the Kid, San Francisco,

Four Seasons Foundation with Dave Haselwood Books, 1968

MUSCLED APPLE SWIFT, Los Angeles, Love Press, 1968

GRAHHR APRIL GRHARRR APRIL, Buffalo, NY, Gallery Upstairs Press, 1968

(poster)

Childhood Memories Are Like the Smallness, London, Cape Goliard Press, 1968

(broadside)

Charles Olson *Call Me Ishmael*, New York, Reynal and Hitchcock, 1947;

Grove, 1958

To Corrado Cagli, New York, Knoedler Gallery, 1947 (poetry)

Y and X, Washington, DC, Black Sun Press, 1948 (poems by Charles Olson,

drawings by Carrado Cagli)

Letter for Melville, Melville Society, Williams College, 1951 (poetry)

This, Black Mountain College, NC, 1952 (poem, design by Nicola Cernovich)

The Maximus Poems 1–10, Stuttgart, Jargon Society, 1953

The Maximus Poems 11–22, Stuttgart, Jargon Society, 1956

In Cold Hell, In Thicket, Dorchester, MA, 1953; Four Seasons Foundation, 1967

The Mayan Letters (ed. Robert Creeley), Majorca, Divers Press, 1953

Anecdotes of the Late War, Highlands, NC, Jargon Society, 1955

O'Ryan 2.4.6.8.10., Berkeley, CA, White Rabbit Press, 1958

Projective Verse, Totem Press, 1959 (essay)

The Maximus Poems, New York, Jargon/Corinth, 1960

The Distances, New York, Grove, 1961

Maximus, from Dogtown – 1. With a foreword by Michael McClure, San Francisco,
     Auerhahn Society, 1961

A Bibliography on America for Ed Dorn, Bolinas, CA, Four Seasons Foundation, 1964

Human Universe and Other Essays (ed. Donald Allen) San Francisco, CA,
     Auerhahn Society, 1965

Proprioception, San Francisco, Four Seasons Foundation, 1965

Stocking Cap, Grabhorn-Hoyem, 1966; Four Seasons Foundation, trade edition,
     1966 (story)

Charles Olson Reading at Berkeley, San Francisco, Coyote, 1966

West, London, Cape Goliard Press, 1966

Selected Writings (ed. Robert Creeley), New York, New Directions, 1967

The Maximus Poems IV, V, VI, London, Cape Goliard Press, 1968

Pleistocene Man: Letters from Charles Olson to John Clarke during October 1965,
     Buffalo, Institute for Further Studies, 1968

'"Volume 0" of a Curriculum for the Study of the Soul', *Letters for Origin,
     1950–1956*, London, Cape Goliard Press, 1969

Ken Weaver (Fugs albums)

The Village Fugs, Folkways Records, Broadside BR-304, 1965 (later issued as
     The Fugs First Album, ESP-Disk, ESP-1018, 1966)

The Fugs, ESP-Disk, ESP-1028, 1966

The Virgin Fugs, ESP-Disk, ESP-1038, 1967

Tenderness Junction, Reprise, RS-6280, 1968

It Crawled Into My Hand, Honest, Reprise, RS-6305, 1968

The Belle of Avenue A, Reprise, RS-6359, 1969

Notes

PREQUEL

1 Geoffrey and Brenda Giuliano, *The Lost Beatles Interviews*, London, Virgin, 1995, p. 224.

2 Jann Wenner (ed.), *Lennon Remembers*, San Francisco, Straight Arrow, p. 29.

CHAPTER 1

1 Paul McCartney, recorded conversation with the author, 4 November 1993.

2 Paul McCartney, recorded conversation with the author, 4 November 1993.

3 Paul McCartney, recorded conversation with the author, early December 1966.

CHAPTER 2

1 Paul McCartney interviewed by David Pearson: *The Sixties*, RSO / Channel 4, 1982; television documentary series.

CHAPTER 3

1 *Survey of London, Volume XXXII: The Parish of St James Westminster, Part Two, North of Piccadilly*, London, Athlone Press, University of London, 1963.

2 Paul McCartney in conversation with the author, 1991 (tape 19 for *Many Years from Now*).

CHAPTER 4

1 Tony Bramwell, *Magical Mystery Tours*, London, Robson, 2005, p. 295.

2 John Lennon interviewed by Jann Wenner, *Rolling Stone*, Nos 74 and 75, 21 January and 4 February 1971.

3 William S. Burroughs in conversation with the author, June 1972.

4 Peter Brown, *The Love You Make*, London, Macmillan, 1986, p. 216.

5 Tony Bramwell, *Magical Mystery Tours*, p. 264.

6 Derek Taylor, *As Time Goes By*, San Francisco, Straight Arrow, 1973, p. 347.

7 Derek Taylor, *As Time Goes By*, p. 347.

8 Peter Asher interviewed in *Rolling Stone*, No. 255, 29 December 1977.

CHAPTER 5

1 David Dalton, 'The Day the Angels Spent Christmas with the Beatles' in
   Gadfly Online, www.gadflyonline.com, accessed September 2014.

2 Ken Kesey, *Demon Box*, New York, Viking, pp. 284–9.

3 Ken Kesey, *Demon Box*, pp. 284–9.

4 Peter Brown, *The Love You Make*, p. 286.

5 Richard DiLello, *The Longest Cocktail Party*, London, Charisma, 1973, p. 89.

6 Tony Bramwell, *Magical Mystery Tours*, p. 300.

7 Tony Bramwell, *Magical Mystery Tours*, p. 299.

CHAPTER 7

1 Charles Olson, *Maximus Poems IV, V, VI*, London, Cape Goliard Press, 1968.

2 Charles Olson, *The Mayan Letters*, London, Cape Editions, 1968.

3 Charles Olson, *Charles Olson Reads From Maximus IV, V, VI*, Folkways Records
   album FL-9738, 1975 (produced by Barry Miles).

CHAPTER 10

1 Letter: Richard Brautigan to Barry Miles, 14 October 1968.

2 Letter: Sarah Fenwick to Richard Brautigan, 22 October 1968.

3 The box labels, with my timings handwritten on them, are illustrated on
   www.brautigan.net/recordings.html and show how much he moved the tracks
   around before he found a satisfactory order.

4 Letter: Richard Brautigan to Barry Miles, 26 April 1969.

CHAPTER 12

1 Richard DiLello, *The Longest Cocktail Party*, p. 163.

CHAPTER 13

1 Cited at John Lennon Discography, www.homepage.ntlworld.com/carousel/ pob/pob04.html, accessed November 2014.

2 Andy Peebles, *The Lennon Tapes: John Lennon and Yoko Ono in Conversation with Andy Peebles, 6 December 1980*, London, BBC, 1981, pp. 19–21.

3 Quoted in Anthony Fawcett, *John Lennon, One Day at a Time*, London, New English Library, 1976, p. 43.

4 Leonard Feather, *Encyclopedia of Jazz in the Sixties*, New York, Horizon, 1966, p. 271.

5 Conversation between Barry Miles, John Lennon and Yoko Ono, 23 and 24 September 1969.

6 Keith Badman, *The Beatles Off the Record*, London, Omnibus, 2000, p. 447.

7 Andy Peebles, *The Lennon Tapes*, p. 19.

CHAPTER 14

1 Dhani Harrison, 'Electronic Sound', in the booklet accompanying the *Electronic Sound* CD in George Harrison, *The Apple Years 1968–75* box set.

2 Quoted at http://www.beatlelinks.net/forums/archive/index.php/t-11367.html, accessed January 2015.

3 Bernie Krause, *Into a Wild Sanctuary*, Berkeley, CA, 1998, p. 62.

4 Bernie Krause, *Into a Wild Sanctuary*, p. 63.

CHAPTER 15

1 Paul McCartney to the author, 16 June 1994.

CHAPTER 16

1 'Nothing Like You' on *Sorcerer* (1967).

2 This must have been the Charles Mingus Quintet: Bill Hardman (trumpet), Jimmy Vass (alto saxophone), Charles McPherson (alto saxophone, flute), Charles Mingus (bass) and Dannie Richmond (drums).

CHAPTER 17

1 Colin Marshall on www.openculture.com, accessed January 2015.

CHAPTER 18

1 Conversation between Barry Miles, John Lennon and Yoko Ono, 23 and 24 September 1969.

Bibliography

Beatles, *The Beatles: An Anthology*, San Francisco, Chronicle Books, 2000

Bramwell, Tony, *Magical Mystery Tours: My Life with the Beatles*, New York, Thomas Dunne, 2005

Brautigan, Ianthe, *You Can't Catch Death: A Daughter's Memoir*, New York, St Martin's, 2000

Brown, Peter and Steve Gaines, *The Love You Make: An Insider's Story of the Beatles*, New York, McGraw-Hill, 1983

Charters, Ann, *Beats and Company: Portrait of a Literary Generation*, Garden City, New York, Dolphin, 1986

Charters, Ann, *Olson / Melville: A Study in Affinity*, n.p., Oyez, 1968

Cott, Jonathan and David Dalton, *The Beatles Get Back*, London, Apple, 1969

DiLello, Richard, *The Longest Cocktail Party*, London, Charisma, 1973

Fawcett, Anthony, *John Lennon: One Day at a Time, A Personal Biography of the Seventies*, New York, Grove, 1976

Ginsberg, Allen, 'To Young or Old Listeners', sleeve notes to Allen Ginsberg, *Songs of Innocence and Experience by William Blake, Tuned by Allen Ginsberg*, MGM album FTS-3083, 1970

Giuliano, Geoffrey and Brenda, *The Lost Beatles Interviews*, London, Virgin, 1995

Hjortsberg, William, *Jubilee Hitchhiker: The Life and Times of Richard Brautigan*, Berkeley, CA, Counterpoint, 2012

Hopkins, Jerry, *Yoko Ono*, London, Sidgwick and Jackson, 1987

Krause, Bernie, *Into a Wild Sanctuary*, Berkeley, CA, 1998

Lewisohn, Mark, *The Complete Beatles Chronicle*, London, Pyramid, 1992

McCabe, Peter, and Robert D. Schonfeld, *Apple to the Core: The Unmaking of the Beatles*, London, Martin Brian and O'Keeffe, 1972

Miles, Barry, *In the Sixties*, London, Jonathan Cape, 2002

Miles, Barry (untitled), sleeve notes to Charles Bukowski, *At Terror Street and Agony Way*, King Mob Double CD KMOB-2, London, 1993

O'Dell, Chris, *Miss O'Dell*, New York, Touchstone, 2009

O'Dell, Denis, *At the Apple's Core: The Beatles from the Inside*, London, Peter Owen, 2002

Olson, Charles, *Charles Olson Reading at Berkeley*, San Francisco, Coyote, 1966

Olson, Charles, *Maximus Poems IV, V, VI*, London, Cape Goliard Press, 1968

Taylor, Alistair, *Yesterday: The Beatles Remembered*, London, Sidgwick and Jackson, 1988

Taylor, Alistair, *A Secret History*, London, John Blake, 2001

Taylor, Derek, *As Time Goes By: Living in the Sixties*, San Francisco, Straight Arrow, 1973

Taylor, Derek, *It was Twenty Years Ago Today*, London, Bantam/Transworld, 1987

Thomson, Graeme, *George Harrison: Behind the Locked Door*, London, Omnibus, 2013

Picture Credits

With grateful thanks to the following picture contributors for their help, expertise and kind permission to use their images on the following pages:

Barry Miles Collection: pp. 24, 30, 31, 42, 48–9, 51, 88 (bottom), 102, 105, 107, 112, 115, 118–9, 120–1, 128, 141, 142 (top), 152, 158–9, 162, 164, 170, 228, 231, 238, 242, 243, 244, 245.

Getty Images archive (detailed credits for individual images below in brackets): p. 1 (Mike Barnes/Fox Photos/Getty Images), p. 37 (bottom – *Evening Standard*/ Getty Images), p. 74 (*Evening Standard*/Getty Images), p. 96 (Estate of Keith Morris/Redferns), p. 180 (SSPL/Getty Images), pp. 194–5 (Susan Wood/Getty Images), p. 218 (C. Maher/*Daily Express*/Hulton Archive/Getty Images), p. 254 (Hans J. Hoffmann/Ullstein Bild via Getty Images).

International Times: pp. 45, 88 (top).

Courtesy of Jess Ex: p. 60.

John 'Hoppy' Hopkins archive (with special thanks to Emily Mahoney and Flip Jelly): pp. 20, 34, 37 (top), 52, 79, 173.

Mark Naboshek Collection (who kindly allowed us to feature some rare items from his superb collection of Beatles memorabilia): pp. 66, 69, 254.

Michael McInnerney Collection: p. 46.

OZ: p. 223.

Sam Cherry Collection (with special thanks to Dani Tull for allowing us to showcase these rare images, the archive can be accessed at www. samcherryphotographer.com): pp. 142 (top), 143.

The Allen Ginsberg Estate (with grateful thanks for sharing their remastered front sleeve with us ahead of the album's re-release in April 2016): p. 249.

The British Library/Barry Miles Collection (with particular thanks to Helen Melody, whose patience in rummaging through Barry Miles's extensive collection unearthed these treasures): pp. 146–7, 165, 174.

Todd Gunderson (with particular appreciation and thanks for his unbounded enthusiasm for Richard Brautigan and this project): pp. 156–7 (the cover art is copyright of Harvest Records).

Topfoto archive (detailed credits for individual images below in brackets): pp. 64–5 (Jane Bown/Observer/Topfoto), p. 188 (Jak Kilby/ArenaPAL), p. 204 (©2004 Credit: Topfoto/UPP).